# History of Ireland

*An Enthralling Overview of Major Events
and Figures in Irish History*

# Free limited time bonus

We forget 90% of everything that we've read in 7 days...

Get the free printable pdf summary of the book you've read AND much, much more... shhhh...

Enter Your Most Frequently Used Email to Get Started

**DOWNLOAD FREE PDF SUMMARY**

© Enthralling History

Stop for a moment. We have a free bonus set up for you. The problem is this: we forget 90% of everything that we read after 7 days. Crazy fact, right? Here's the solution: we've created a printable, 1-page pdf summary for this book that you're reading now. All you have to do to get your free pdf summary is to go to the following website: **https://livetolearn.lpages.co/enthrallinghistory/**

## Or, Scan the QR code!

Once you do, it will be intuitive. Enjoy, and thank you!

# Table of Contents

# Introduction: Lost Tales from an Irish Past

To say that Irish history is long is perhaps an understatement. The earliest evidence of human habitation is believed to go as far back as 10,500 BCE. It is said that at some distant point in Ireland's prehistory, a group of hunter-gatherers migrated from Scotland and moved into northeastern Ireland during the Stone Age. The archaeological record suggests that the early settlers set up shop in what is now Ireland's Antrim County around the year 6000 BCE.

It is still debated exactly how humans arrived in Ireland. Some scholars have theorized that a land bridge might have existed and that they simply walked across from various parts of Britain. Others insist these settlers sailed across the narrow strait of the North Channel in small makeshift boats.

A few thousand years later, these bold settlers merged with a new wave of Neolithic migrants. This group left huge megalithic monuments similar to England's famous Stonehenge. Many of these monuments can be found scattered about Ireland's County Meath. Just like their more famous contemporary, Stonehenge, these monuments demonstrated a rather advanced understanding of astronomy and how it related to the local environment.

These monuments are located in eastern Ireland's Boyne Valley, a place that is absolutely rich in archaeological evidence. The site has since been dubbed "Newgrange," and the constructed work found there is called the Newgrange monument. It is referred to as such because it was in the vicinity of the "newer" grange (farms) that were utilized by monks from nearby Mellifont Abbey.

The Newgrange monument is thought to have been built by Neolithic farmers around 3200 BCE. The monument stands about 43 feet tall and is around 279 feet in diameter. Interestingly, the interior chambers are constructed in such a way that they are perfectly aligned with the sunrise during the winter solstice. Anyone who happened to walk through the passageway at this time would be greeted by brilliantly illuminating rays of winter sunshine.

Although comparisons have been made to England's Stonehenge, in many ways, this complex is quite similar to the large Native American burial mounds found in North America. It also likely served a similar purpose too, since it is believed this site served as a tomb as well as an astronomical calendar.

These ancient residents of Ireland were quite good at tracking the stars and planets that traversed the skies. Unfortunately, they were not quite so savvy when it came to documenting their own history. As such, much of what has been speculated about them devolves into theories and guesswork. However, the artifacts that they left us clearly indicate they were an intelligent and thoughtful people. They still manage to loom large in tales from a lost Irish past.

# Chapter 1: The Celtic Era: Ancient Ireland

*"Love is never defeated, and I could add, the history of Ireland proves it."*

*-Pope John Paul II*

If one is to consider Ireland's past, it does not take long before the notion of Celtic culture rises to the forefront of one's mind. Even today, the mystique of Celtic culture in Ireland looms large. There is, of course, Celtic music and dance, which has captivated countless souls, not just in Ireland but also all across the globe. The demand for all things Celtic is indeed high today. But when exactly did the actual Celtic era of ancient Ireland begin?

Although the date is not known for sure, it has been suggested that the period of Celtic Ireland began around 1000 BCE. The Celts first hailed from western Europe and from there pushed onward into Ireland.

It seems that the Celts built much of their civilization and culture on what had already been in place, such as the aforementioned Newgrange monument.

**Newgrange.**

This is a perfect example of newcomers making use of an older monument for their own purposes. Historians widely agree that the monuments are so ancient (some speculate that they are even older than the pyramids of Egypt) that they could not have been built by the Celts. Even so, after the Celts moved into the region, they made use of it. The Celts left their own unique signature on this ancient megalithic site by way of Celtic spirals, which can be seen all throughout this megalithic compound.

The Celtic spiral is a piece of artwork that represents the Celtic view of life being cyclical. The Celts felt that everything had a cycle, just like the seasons, which go through repetitive cycles of growth, decay, death, and rebirth. They viewed their lives as being caught up in this repetitive cycle of multiple phases of existence.

The Celts also seem to have co-opted Neolithic gods known as the Tuatha as part of their own beliefs and eventually transformed them into their own deities. From the legends of the Tuatha de Danann, the Irish derived tales of enigmatic little people sometimes referred to as the wee folk, the fair folks, or fairies (also spelled as faeries).

Fairies in Irish folklore can range from J. R. R. Tolkien-styled elves who live in wooded sanctuaries to the leprechaun guarding his pot of gold to menacing goblins or, even worse, the fearsome banshee who haunts our worst nightmares with her cries.

The origin of fairies is not exactly known, but Irish folklore seems to suggest they came from over the sea after an earthquake, leading some to ponder if they could have been shipwrecked survivors from the lost island of Atlantis. Even odder, however, are Irish legends stating that the fairies descended onto the island from so-called "cloud ships."

Yes, that is right. There are legends pointing to the origin of fairies as being from somewhere up in the clouds. These creatures eventually descended down to Earth at some distant point in the past like otherworldly enchanted explorers. The celebrated tale of the "Ever-Living Ones" from Irish folklore famously speaks of the fair folk landing their "cloud" on the Emerald Isle. As one can imagine, proponents of ancient astronaut theory have had a field day with these legends over the years.

The Celts not only made use of these ancient sites, but they also coexisted fairly well with those who were already in place. The Celtic people essentially became a very strong minority in the region. Their influence would rise and fall with the new influxes of other people groups in Ireland. However, this all depended on the region and the people groups present there. The Celts likely experienced periods of peace and war. Eventually, the Celts displaced the native inhabitants, assimilating them or driving them off, allowing the Celts to become the most dominant people group on the island.

The Celtic people's governmental system was based on the monarchy. This was a locally based system, meaning there was not a king of the whole of Ireland, at least at first.

The Celts made use of ring forts to fortify the rule of those charged with stewardship. Each ring fort had its own ruler. These many kings would have a profound influence on Ireland.

One of the more interesting things about this complex monarchy of many rulers was that it was not based on hereditary. It was actually based on an election system.

Ireland would come to have about one hundred of these small kingdoms. These small principalities were then grouped into five larger conglomerates, which would become the basic provinces of Ireland:

Ulster, Meath, Leinster, Munster, and Connacht.

Eventually, the provinces were governed by a so-called "High King," who would be centered in one province but have overarching authority over the others. This system tended to foster much infighting and discord. One potential claimant to the throne of the high king would fight for his position with others, and the coalitions behind the claimants struggled against each other.

This state of affairs often left Ireland in a state of disunity. Even though the warriors of Ireland were fierce and more than ready to fight off Romans, Vikings, and the English, their own lack of unity left them facing constant domestic turmoil.

Interestingly, by the time of the Romans, even though England was placed under the control of the Roman Empire, Ireland was considered out of bounds and not worth the effort. During the days of the Roman Republic, Julius Caesar landed on the southern coast of Britain on two different occasions, once in 55 BCE and again in 54 BCE. However, he never went near Ireland.

According to Roman historian Tacitus, it was not until the middle of the 1st century CE that Ireland was on the minds of the Roman armies. Roman General Gnaeus Julius Agricola (who just so happened to be Tacitus's father-in-law) ranged through the coasts of southern Scotland. At one point, he could see the shores of Ireland in the distance. Tacitus goes on to relate that Agricola claimed that all he needed was a single Roman legion and the authority to use it to easily seize the new land he saw.

Britain had plenty of resources to keep the Romans occupied, such as its lead and tin deposits. Ireland, on the other hand, simply was not viewed as being worth the effort. Ireland did not have the resources the Romans needed. For the most part, the Irish inhabitants did not bother the Romans, although piracy did occur. Why waste perfectly good Roman men in taking an island that, frankly, was not desired?

The Romans had enough on their hands with Britain. They faced multiple uprisings and rebellions in the region. Despite the Romans' best attempts, they never managed to get all of Britain under their control. The Scottish tribes were a particular thorn in the Roman Empire's side. Roman Emperor Hadrian famously built up a wall to demarcate the claimed Roman domain.

It is not entirely clear whether or not the Irish Celts made a habit of raiding Roman sites after the wall was first put up. Writer and historian Paul F. State has speculated as much due to the fact that Roman artifacts dating back to the 1ˢᵗ century CE have been found in Ireland. State has speculated these items might have been stolen from the Romans after Celts raided Roman bases on the frontiers of Roman Britain. However, these items very well could have been received through trade.

There is evidence that the Irish themselves attempted to insert their own colonies in parts of Britain. During the 4ᵗʰ century CE, Irish settlements were established in Wales. The biggest thrust of this Irish invasion force hailed from Leinster, and it is said that the name of the Llyn Peninsula is derived from this fact.

Claims of Irish inroads into Britain are further backed up by a 10ᵗʰ-century chronicle from an Irish bishop and king from County Tipperary, who once made the following claim:

"The power of the Irish over the Britons was great, and they had divided Britain between them into estates ... And the Irish lived as much east of the sea as they did in Ireland, and their dwellings and royal fortresses were made there ... And they were in that control for a long time even after the coming of St. Patrick to Ireland."

If this account is to be believed, it sounds like powerful Irish rulers were cavorting back and forth over the Irish sea with ease. The way the chronicler puts it, Irish power players were setting up shop in northern Britain with their "dwellings and royal fortresses" and basically lording it over the locals as much as they could.

Celtic pirates were problematic at times for the Romans and native Britons. These pirates targeted coastal towns, villages, and trading ships. They sought riches, livestock, slaves, and valuable commodities, such as precious metals, textiles, and foodstuffs. One of the most famous slaves the Celtic pirates captured was none other than Saint Patrick.

The Celts, in general, were skilled seafarers and warriors. They used fast and maneuverable vessels, which allowed them to swiftly approach their targets, conduct surprise attacks, and evade pursuit. Despite lacking advanced navigation tools, they were still remarkable navigators. They observed the skies, landmarks, currents, and winds to navigate the seas.

In ancient Ireland, Celtic society was organized into a hierarchical structure, with warriors occupying a prominent position. Warriors were highly esteemed for their bravery, skill in combat, and loyalty to their leaders. They underwent rigorous training from a young age, learning combat techniques, weapon proficiency, and tactics. The most popular Celtic weapons were swords, spears, javelins, shields, and bows and arrows. Celtic warriors employed various tactics. They were known for their skill in close combat, and they often relied on hit-and-run tactics or ambushes to get the upper hand.

The Celtic tribes were known for their warrior spirit and fierce independence, which gave the Romans pause when it came to invading Ireland. The Romans nearly launched an invasion of Ireland proper. Plans were made in 81 CE by an ambitious Roman general—the aforementioned Agricola—only for the plans to be canceled by a doubtful Emperor Domitian, who considered the venture too risky and not worth the effort.

Domitian realized he would need quite a bit of manpower for such a feat and prudently understood that Rome's legions were stretched too thin as it was. He recognized that he needed those troops at the ready should other fires erupt on other Roman frontiers.

Even so, the influence of Rome could still be felt in Ireland, even if the island was not being actively occupied by Roman troops. Coins, for example, dating back to the reign of the aforementioned Hadrian (r. 117 CE–138 CE) are still being found scattered along the eastern shores of the Irish coast. Once again, historians debate whether these coins were received through trade or raid, but either way, the influence of the Romans is clear.

The Romans give us our first glimpses into the Irish historical record. The Celts in Ireland had a written language (Ogham), but it is not clear when this language was created. Most scholars believe it was invented in the 4th century CE, while others insist it was created in the 1st century BCE. If the latter is true, the Celts either did not keep written records due to a strong belief in oral traditions or these records were destroyed. Nevertheless, their strong oral tradition allowed their history and legends to be recorded, although this occurred much later. And as we know, things get lost or misconstrued when written down centuries after the fact.

Many of these oral legends speak of powerful Irish kings. One of the most famous of these kings was a figure named Cormac mac Airt (sometimes also spelled as Cormac ua Conn). Although it is debated, some scholars—historian Paul F. State being one of them—believed that he was a real king who lived during the $3^{rd}$ century.

It is said that Cormac mac Airt held court in the ancient Irish city of Tara and had a large army of Fianna, an elite military guard made up of warriors who hailed from the Irish nobility. If true, this powerful Irish king of legend would have lived during one of the most pivotal times in both Irish and Roman history. He would have reigned over Ireland just as the Romans were bumping shoulders right up against (but not into) his Irish domain.

At any rate, rather than foreign conquering armies, it would be foreign cultural innovations and, more importantly, philosophical outlooks that would penetrate deep into the Irish world. In the $4^{th}$ century CE, the Roman Empire underwent a massive conversion to Christianity. It would not be long before missionaries from the Roman Catholic Church arrived on Irish shores.

# Chapter 2: The Arrival of Christianity

*"I am Patrick, a sinner and very ignorant man. I declare that I have been appointed as a bishop in Ireland—and I believe that I have received this position from God himself. I live as a stranger and exile here among barbarians and pagans because of my love for God. He is my witness that this is true. I have never wanted to speak harshly and sternly, but the zeal of God and the truth of Christ have forced me to do it for the sake of my neighbors and children, for whom I gave up my homeland, my family, and my very life until my death. I live for my God to teach unbelievers, if I am worthy, even if some people hate me."*

*-Saint Patrick*

Interestingly, even though it was England who benefited the most from Roman occupation, with the people there enjoying paved roads, efficient methods of government, and Roman laws, Ireland would become the center of the Roman Catholic faith. After the fall of the Roman Empire, Ireland's backwardness and lack of roads actually enabled it to become a kind of refuge for Christianity.

Unlike much of the world at the time, Ireland was hard to reach and, therefore, hard to threaten. Christian missionaries first began to make trips to Ireland in the $3^{rd}$ century, but it was a $5^{th}$-century missionary by the name of Patrick who would make the biggest inroads.

Patrick hailed from a wealthy Roman family. He was the son of a Roman magistrate by the name of Calpurnius. Calpurnius was also apparently a deacon in the local church where Patrick grew up. Patrick was likely poised to follow in his father's footsteps when fate intervened. As a young man, Patrick was kidnapped by a group of Irish pirates.

Kidnapping wealthy young Romans had been a tradition about as old as Rome itself. One of the most famous Roman rulers, Julius Caesar, had even been kidnapped by pirates, although this happened hundreds of years before Saint Patrick's time. Typically, the kidnappers wanted money from the wealthy relatives of those they had taken. Once a ransom was paid, they would release the people they held in captivity.

But in the case of Patrick, his captors were not looking for ransom. Instead, they sold him off to the highest bidder. Patrick was purchased and enslaved. He was made to work as a shepherd for six years before he finally escaped. After he had returned, Patrick shocked his friends and family by deciding to return to Ireland of his own free will as a missionary.

According to some accounts, he supposedly heard a voice telling him, "We beseech you to come and walk amongst us once more." Patrick understood this as a direct command to go back to Ireland to preach the gospel and that was what he did. He arrived back in Ireland in 432 CE and used the rest of his time on Earth preaching to the Irish.

He would spend around thirty years in Ireland, preaching the gospel throughout the Emerald Isle. He not only achieved to attract many converts to the faith, but he also established churches that would remain lasting focal points for the religion, as well as the larger society as a whole. By the time of Saint Patrick's passing, churches could be found all across the Irish landscape.

One of the reasons for Saint Patrick's success was his deep understanding of Ireland, its people, its civic structure, and its culture. Patrick was a keen observer, and during his captivity in Ireland, he had learned much. He put this knowledge of the inner workings of Ireland to good use when he set about establishing a lasting Christian foothold.

For example, Patrick understood the nature of multiple rulers in multiple regions ruled by an overarching high king. He did not seek to disrupt this system. On the contrary, he worked carefully within its framework and made adjustments when necessary so that the churches he established could exist in harmony with local leadership.

Saint Patrick was especially in good with the leaders of Armagh. Armagh is an ancient city in Ireland that dates back to at least the 1$^{st}$

century CE. It was a sacred site for pagan worshipers. In Patrick's day, Armagh was still viewed as a site of significance, so it only made sense for him to try and make it a focal point for Irish Catholicism.

The fact that Saint Patrick had ingratiated himself with the leaders of Armagh primed this region to become very prominent in the Irish Church; this prominence is still firmly intact to this very day. The city of Armagh itself would become the centerpiece of St. Patrick's mission, with his efforts spreading out in a circle from there.

Following in Saint Patrick's example, many Irish bishops maintained close relationships with the most important ruling families of Ireland. Soon, the church structure of Ireland is said to have basically "mirrored" the civic structure that was already in place.

Saint Patrick and his contemporaries were also keen not to try to excise much of the already existing Irish culture and folklore. As long as the native beliefs could be made somewhat compatible or, at the very least, did not present a significant threat to the Christian religion, Patrick and his immediate contemporaries did not seem to trouble themselves too much with the fact that Irish Christians still believed in fairies and leprechauns.

There is a rather persistent legend that Saint Patrick drove the snakes from Ireland. He supposedly stood on top of a hill and ordered the snakes to leave; true believers still insist that they did. Most scholars believe this is a myth, though. Geologists back up the sheer impossibility of this divine task, not because Saint Patrick was not up for it but because it is not believed Ireland ever had snakes to begin with.

It is believed that after the ice retreated from the last Ice Age, the subsequent Irish Sea that separates Ireland from Britain presented too formidable a barrier for any snakes to cross. Although this theorized reason for Ireland being snake-free is often presented (for lack of a better term) as gospel, we would be wise to remember that it is still just a theory. If people wish to believe that Saint Patrick is the reason Ireland has no snakes, they will likely hold fast to their own theory as well.

Another interesting thing about the Christianization of Ireland is the way that it allowed local traditions to integrate with Christian ideas. For example, missionaries like Patrick pointed to Ireland's celebrated three-leaf clovers (shamrocks) as an example of the Trinity.

According to legend, it is said that Saint Patrick spoke of how the shamrock sprouted three leaves from the same source just like God, who was a triune entity that likewise emerged from the same eternal source.

Saint Patrick was speaking of complex subjects to the Irish, so the utilization of a familiar visual aid in the form of a shamrock likely would have made a lot more sense to them. We do not have firm evidence that this comparison happened, but if Saint Patrick or any other Roman Catholic missionary did such a thing, it really would not be surprising. There are examples of these sorts of attempts to bridge perceived cultural divides all throughout Christian history.

Christianity introduced much that Ireland had been lacking in terms of civilization. Christianity finally introduced a viable writing system to the Irish. It is true that the Celts had their own runic system, but it was not well established, and Celtic runes could hardly compete with the Latin alphabet that the Christians brought with them.

Due to this influx of Christian high learning, as well as the relative seclusion of Ireland, Ireland became an unlikely safeguard of culture and civilization after the fall of the Roman Empire and throughout the so-called Dark Ages.

Saint Patrick was keen to encourage monastic life. Several monasteries and countless monks, who were dedicated to studying the Bible in seclusion, began to pop up all over Ireland. These monasteries were not only centers of learning but also—as we will dive into a bit more in depth shortly—important focal points of civic society. The monasteries created a solid set of rules by which the surrounding communities would come to live.

St. Kevin's Monastery in Wicklow County built in the 500s.
*Schcambo at English Wikipedia, CC BY 3.0 <https://creativecommons.org/licenses/by/3.0>, via Wikimedia Commons; https://commons.wikimedia.org/wiki/File:Glendalough_monastery.jpg*

These monks were not always shut up in their monasteries either. They periodically went around to preach the gospel and generally did their best to keep the flame of Christianity alive.

The Irish even managed to revitalize Christianity in western Europe when it was in decline. Ireland paid back the missionary favor by sending homegrown saints abroad, such as the bold and eloquent Columba, who left Ireland in the 6ᵗʰ century.

Columba was born in 521 in County Donegal in Ulster. During his time in Ireland, he planted many monasteries and aided his fellow believers in any way he could. He would leave Ireland to preach abroad in 563.

It is easy to assume that his sudden departure was due to his own zeal to spread the gospel, but according to historians, it was actually a bit more complicated than that. There is no doubt that religious zeal to evangelize was a part of it, but there were some other factors at work as well.

Just prior to leaving Ireland, Columba had gotten into a major row with the local powers that be over a prized manuscript (some traditions suggest it was the Vulgate/Latin translation of the scripture) that he had apparently copied without authorization.

The other main job of monks in monasteries was to serve as scribes. Prior to the invention of the printing press, many monks spent much of their entire lives painstakingly copying books and other written texts by hand.

This is apparently what Columba did with the document in question. Another member of the Irish clergy, Saint Finian, was not too happy about it. Upon learning of Columba's unauthorized copying, he ordered him to hand over the document.

Finnian was so irate he took the matter up with the high king of Ireland, Diarmait mac Cerbaill. Both Finnian and Columba ended up taking their case before the king. Finnian argued that it was wrong for Columba to copy the manuscript without his permission, whereas Columba argued that it was wrong for Finnian to try and hold the scripture hostage. Columba basically argued that the document should be accessible to everyone and that he or anyone else should be able to copy it at any time.

Intriguing to think that such arguments were being made before the modern notion of copyright infringement existed. The high king used his own common sense to formulate a ruling on the matter. He supposedly reasoned that just as a calf belongs to a cow, a copy of a book belongs to the original owner of the book. The high king decided that it was indeed Saint Columba who was in the wrong.

This ruling caused much rancor between Columba and High King Diarmait mac Cerbaill. Some historians believe that Columba might have taken his overseas evangelizing mission as a kind of "penance" for the distress that had erupted. If anything, it was likely a good excuse just to get away from all of the drama.

Whatever the case may be, he left with twelve fellow pilgrims. Columba's first stop on this journey was the island of Iona, just west of Scotland. This monastery would go on to become a celebrated site for pilgrims, but upon his arrival, it was ground zero for an ideological battle between Irish Christians and pagans for it was here that he encountered those who were of the Druid faith.

Druidism dates back to some point in antiquity. The first real mention of them was by Julius Caesar, who encountered Celtic Druids during the first ill-fated Roman invasion of Britain. Caesar's most prominent recollection of this mysterious religion was that it engaged in a form of human sacrifice. It has been said that Druids would put people inside giant wicker statues and burn them alive as a sacrifice to their deities.

Columba apparently encountered some of the Druid holdouts and did everything he could to convert those who still practiced Druidism. He also sought to convert local leaders among the Picts, a predominant people group in the region at the time. Columba was successful in this aim, as he managed to persuade King Brude of the Picts into becoming a Christian.

By the time of Columba's death in 597, he had reached much of Scotland, as well as northern England. His influence even managed to extend as far afield as the Orkney Islands.

By this point, the Western Roman Empire had long since fallen, and much of western Europe was in upheaval. The fact that Columba and his followers were able to carry on the message of Roman Catholicism, even once the Western Roman Empire was no more, stands as a great testament of the strength of the Irish brand of Christianity. The calm steady hand of Columba did much to steward a battered and weary flock through these difficult times.

As mentioned, monasteries served as a focal point for societal change in the surrounding cultures. In 697, about one hundred years after Columba's passing, a conference of bishops led by a priest named Adomnan of Iona hashed out the "Law of Innocents." This law instituted important safeguards for women and children

For example, the law insisted that children should not be turned into child soldiers and forced to fight in wars. The law also stipulated that women should not be assaulted and subjected to violence. We would likely consider such things as a given in modern times, but without the influence of these bishops in making sure these basic human rights were enforced, this might not have been the case back then.

Interestingly, the law also covered Christian priests themselves. Along with women and children, clerics were considered innocent non-combatants who should not be forced into altercations.

Saint Patrick wrote at length about the protection of innocent life back in his day. In one of his letters, which has managed to survive throughout the centuries, he speaks passionately about some of the terrible loss of life he had witnessed. This epistle, which was entitled "Letter to the Soldiers of Coroticus," was aimed at a particular British ruler whose soldiers had severely transgressed against some of his flock.

In the letter, Patrick stated:

"I have composed and written these words with my own hand, to be taken, sent, and delivered to the soldiers of Coroticus. I don't call them my countrymen or blessed Roman citizens, because by their evil deeds they have become fellow citizens with demons. They act in the same way as our enemies and live in death as allies of the Irish and the apostate Picts. They are blood-thirsty men yearning for the blood of innocent Christians, the very ones I brought to life in God and confirmed in Christ. The day after these men cruelly cut down with their swords my newly baptized—they were still clothed in their white garments and had anointing oil on their foreheads—I sent a letter to them by the hand of a holy priest I had trained since his youth, along with some clerics. I asked that they return the baptized captives along with some of the goods they had stolen, but they laughed at them. I don't know who I should weep for more, whether it be the ones killed, those captured, or the men trapped so completely in the devil's snares. For whoever commits sin is the slave of sin and will be known as a child of the devil."

Saint Patrick was disgusted with the wanton violence he saw in Ireland, and he went on to state:

"So let all who fear God know that these men are strangers to me and to Christ my God, the one I serve as an ambassador. They are murderers of fathers and brothers, ravaging wolves who devour the people of God as if they were bread. As scripture says: 'The wicked have destroyed your law, O Lord,' the same law that our merciful and kind God has established in Ireland in these last days."

It is interesting to note the apocalyptic tone that Saint Patrick takes. Christians have been stating that the end is near ever since the very beginning of the faith. Even though no date has ever been officially set, the Bible states that the end could come at any moment and to watch and wait for certain signs.

Saint Patrick also claimed that he had the authority to voice his concerns about violence, saying, "I am not exceeding my authority for I am one of those men God has called and predestined to preach the gospel in the face of terrible persecutions to the very ends of the Earth, even if our enemy shows his jealousy through the tyrant Coroticus, a man with no respect for God or his priests. For God has chosen priests and given them the greatest, most divine, and sublime power, so that whoever they bind on Earth, they will also be bound in heaven."

Patrick is saying that, just like the pope, he holds an important office. And thanks to the efforts of Saint Patrick and others, the church became a predominant focal point of the Irish world at this time.[1] During much of the 7th and 8th centuries, the church would be the center of rule-making, education, and the economy.

The great castle-like monasteries stored up tremendous amounts of treasure. As writer and historian Peter Neville put it, "The great monasteries of the day, rather than the kings and princelings who fought for domination throughout the pre-Viking period, were the main economic units in this society. A great monastery like Durrow could have many thousands of tenants, dependent churches with their estates, and vast wealth."[2]

---

[1] An interesting side note here is that Patrick has never been formally canonized by a pope. Nevertheless, many Christians refer to Patrick as Saint Patrick.

[2] Neville, Peter. *A Traveller's History of Ireland.* 1992.

Because of this, the bishop was considered a ruler of sorts, ruling over his own monastic kingdom. The secular leaders of Ireland tended to work hand in hand with the clergy. They expected the clergy to essentially serve as representatives of the communities where they served.

The notion that bishops would serve a dual purpose as community leaders was realized by none other than Saint Patrick and was duly noted in the so-called "Riaghail Phatraic" ("Law of Patrick").

Scholar Peter Neville went into some detail about this in his book *A Traveller's History of Ireland.* As Peter Neville noted, this particular bit of monastic legislation decreed, "There shall be a chief bishop of each tuath to ordain their clergy, to consecrate their churches, to be confessor to rulers and superiors, and to sanctify and bless their children after baptism."

It really should not be surprising that such a hierarchy might have been established. The pope, after the fall of the Western Roman Empire, was basically considered the ruler of his own realm. Even today, the pope is considered the head of his own miniature realm within Rome, now known as Vatican City.

The "Law of Patrick" acknowledged such an arrangement and sought to reproduce it on a smaller scale in Ireland, with the bishops ruling their own small monastic domains. Since the bishops were considered rulers in their own right, the monastery was a kind of nerve center for the community. They were intermediaries between the commoners and the rulers of Ireland. With no army of their own, these monastic domains were the soft underbelly of Irish administration. It probably should not surprise us that invaders such as the Vikings would choose to attack them.

Ruthless bands of Vikings would swoop down on Ireland, entirely disregarding the "Law of Innocents" as they killed many they encountered, robbed monasteries of their treasure, and did their best to strike fear in the hearts of those they encountered. The Vikings were a scary bunch, and their arrival would alter the course of Irish Christianity in many profound and unpredictable ways.

With the arrival of the Vikings, Ireland's relative peace and prosperity would come to an abrupt end when the Irish were hit with an entirely unexpected onslaught from the north. Their antagonists could care less about Christianity. In their opinion, it would have been just fine if the religion were snuffed out entirely (although their feelings about the religion would change as time passed).

# Chapter 3: Viking Invasions in Early Medieval Ireland

*"The Irish do not want anyone to wish them well—they want everyone to wish their enemies ill."*

*-Harold Nicolson*

As much as Ireland might have been a refuge for Christianity and learning during the Dark Ages, that relative sense of security would come to a shocking end when Vikings from the cold north launched an unexpected and devastating attack on a Christian monastery in Lindisfarne. The attack occurred in 793 CE on the actual island of Lindisfarne, which is situated just off the coastlines of Northumberland.

While the island is not part of Ireland, it has a long Irish tradition. In 635 CE, St. Aidan, an Irish monk, founded Lindisfarne Monastery. The monastery became a center of great learning. Around 700 CE, a beautiful illuminated Latin manuscript known as the Lindisfarne Gospels was written.

At the time, the attack seemed entirely random. The monks had certainly done nothing to offend these strangers. So, why did it occur? Well, the targeting of Lindisfarne might not have been as random as was once thought. Lindisfarne was a major center of Christian outreach in the region. One of the groups being actively targeted by this outreach was, no doubt, some of the Vikings, who resided farther north in the lands of Scandinavia.

Some scholars believe the Vikings were in the midst of a kind of holy war with the Catholic Church. Prior to this attack on Lindisfarne, Charlemagne the Great, King of the Franks and Lombards, sent an expedition into what is now Denmark and butchered the Norse pagans he found there. He also ordered his troops to burn down one of their sacred trees.

This incident occurred in 772 when Charlemagne's forces were pushing deeper and deeper into what was then known as Saxony. This sacred tree (or pillar) was known as an Irminsul.

It is worth noting that Norse mythology, as well as the Druid mythology of Ireland, places a special emphasis on sacred trees. If it is ever cut down, the Vikings believe Ragnarök (the Norse version of Armageddon) would occur. In Norse mythology, Yggdrasil is a great tree that symbolically represents the universe itself. The Latin variation of Irminsul, in fact, is *universalis columna*, which basically means "column that carries the universe."

When Irminsul, a representation of Yggdrasil, was destroyed, many Vikings took this as a sign that the end times had begun. And it was shortly after all of this that Lindisfarne was burned to the ground.

Could it be a coincidence? There is still a lot of debate on this, but it is plausible that, that from the Viking perspective, pillaging and burning Lindisfarne was just as much one of vengeance as it was for mere plunder.

However, it is incredibly likely that the Vikings chose Lindisfarne because it was isolated and presented an easy target to raid. The attack sent shockwaves through the Christian community. How could anyone kill monks and pillage relics and treasures from a religious center? As has been mentioned, the Vikings followed a different religion, so they obviously did not hold Christianity in as high of a regard. To them, treasure was treasure.

Regardless of why the attack on Lindisfarne happened, Viking attacks increased over the years. Ireland was not spared.

Ireland had long been domestically divided by a system of many kings who were ruled by one high king. The country had its weaknesses, especially disunity. One of the early efforts to thwart these devastating Viking raids was to build a series of watch towers in and around monasteries and other vulnerable installations.

These watch towers provided an eagle-eye view of any approach so that the alarm could be raised. The towers were formidable fortresses and could also serve as places of refuge if need be.

The Vikings, however, were playing for keeps. They soon moved from random raids to launching all-out invasions. The first wave of these occurred in 795. Fast forward to around 836, and the Vikings were launching major inland expeditions.

The Vikings continued to force their way into Ireland until they began to seize tracts of land and settle in the region. It was thanks to the Vikings that the fortified cities of Dublin, Wexford, Waterford, Cork, and Limerick were developed. The Vikings, as fierce as their penchant for fighting was, proved to be great administrators. They quickly turned their settlements into major hubs of commercial trade.

This was most especially the case in Dublin. According to historian Peter F. State, the oldest records of a Viking settlement in the region first emerged in 843 CE. Crude but sturdy structures were erected on the banks of the Liffey River. These likely began as a staging area for Vikings arriving from the north. The Vikings sailed down into the Irish Sea and then into what is now called Dublin Bay, which is the mouth of the Liffey River.

This settlement was soon fortified with earthen barriers and even stone walls. These fortifications allowed Viking ships to come and go with ease, and both raiding and trading was pushed farther inland into the rest of Ireland.

The Vikings thrived and continued to take advantage of the disorganized state of the native Irish. Yet, paradoxically enough, it has been said that it was the very disorganized and decentralized nature of the Irish state that might have spared it from a complete Viking takeover. If there had been just one centralized ruler of Ireland, it would have been pretty easy for a huge Viking army to descend, knock out the power base, and then take over. Without a single centralized ruler, the Vikings had several fires they had to put out at the same time.

Even so, the Irish would soon rally behind one of their own who promised to get rid of the Vikings once and for all. Around the year 1000, a powerful Irish leader by the name of Brian Boru arrived on the scene.

Brian Boru was a skilled leader and warrior who managed to battle his way to the top of Ireland's power structure. Brian was practically born into a state of warfare with his father, Cennetig's, family—the Dal Cais dynasty—duking it out with the Eoganacht dynasty of Munster. Cennetig was successful in this aim, and by the time he perished in 951, his sons, Mathgamain and Brian Boru, were able to continue the push deeper into Munster.

Mathgamain was double-crossed by his defeated foes, and he died in 976. This left Brian in charge of his family's conquest of Ireland. He did not disappoint, as he soon had control of all of Munster, located in southern Ireland. He then turned his attention to the north, to Ulster. Here, he put down several smaller kings before his attention was turned to Leinster and the Viking stronghold of Dublin.

In 999, Brian Boru managed to put down his most powerful rivals in Leinster and Dublin. By the year 1011, Brian Boru's dominance over Ireland was all but secured. However, it would soon become clear that there was still some unsettled business to take care of. The king of Leinster, Máel Mórda mac Murchada, had already given his submission but simmered with resentment. Once Brian Boru's back was turned, Mael Morda entered into a plot with the Vikings to align his forces with the Viking warlord Jarl Sigurd of Orkney.

In 1014, the Battle of Clontarf was waged just outside of Dublin on Good Friday. A coalition of Irish warriors assembled by Brian Boru smashed into this new threat. Brian Boru was killed in the battle, but his nemesis and rival, Máel Mórda mac Murchada, was also killed. The Vikings in Ireland had been dealt a decisive blow.

However, even though the Vikings were defeated at Clontarf, they remained very much in place. From that moment forward, they would continue the long, drawn-out process of intermingling with the locals. There would be intermarriage and the merging of customs. As historian Paul F. State contends, this new unique phase of Irish culture could be referred to as being "Hiberno-Norse." This blend of cultures and traditions would ultimately stand up to the onslaught of an impending invasion from Normandy, France.

# Chapter 4: The Norman Conquest and the Start of Anglo Control

*"You that would judge me, do not judge alone this book or that, come to this hallowed place where my friends' portraits hang and look thereon. Ireland's history in their lineaments trace; think where my glory most begins and ends and say my glory was I had such friends."*

*-William Butler Yeats*

The Norman invasion is usually viewed as an invasion of Britain. However, Ireland also faced an invasion, which occurred in May 1169. The Normans, as it turns out, had the same problem that the Vikings had before them.

The Normans very much would have liked to have achieved a knockout blow as they had in England by defeating the high king of Ireland in battle. However, Ireland was once again in a state of disunity during this time, so there was no sole authority figure for the Normans to topple. Even so, the Norman war machine continued to move forward with plans for the seizure of Ireland.

In consideration of all of this, it must be asked what was in it for the Normans. Why did they go to all of the trouble to invade Ireland in the first place?

It seems that one of the primary motivations was that Ireland, despite its general disunity, boasted a robust trade network, which dated all the way back to the times of the Vikings. This makes sense; after all, the Vikings had turned Dublin into a major trading hub. Dublin was the center of a network that had arms spiraling out as far as Bristol.

Prior to the Norman invasion of Ireland, the Norman invasion of England was led by one of history's most renowned and iconic figures: William the Conqueror. Prior to conquering England, he held the title of the duke of Normandy.

The drama began when the English king, Edward the Confessor, abruptly perished in 1066 without a clear heir to the throne. William was ready to stake a claim since Richard II of Normandy, the deceased King Edward's uncle, was his grandfather.

However, this claim was not recognized in England, and a noble named Harold Godwinson was made king instead. After the English refused to recognize William's claim, he decided to take over by force. This led to a Norman landing and the subsequent Battle of Hastings on October 14th, 1066. This fateful battle would leave Harold dead on the battlefield and his troops defeated. William still had some more fighting to do, but before the year was out, he would be hailed as king. He was officially crowned on Christmas Day (December 25th), 1066.

William the Conqueror would perish in 1087, but his Norman successors led the charge into Ireland. Between the years 1169 and 1171, the Normans managed to score several wins against the Irish.

During this period, all of southeastern Ireland was besieged, and Wexford was taken by the Normans. The Normans and their English auxiliaries were aided in their conquest by superior equipment. The Norman armies were outfitted with the latest weapons and armor, whereas the Irish armaments were typically second-rate.

The Norman and English troops, for example, had formidable crossbows, which they used to decimate Irish infantry. The Irish, on the other hand, were still using primitive slings to hurl rocks at their opponents. As writer and historian Peter Neville put it, "The Normans had heavily-mailed knights who fought on horseback and were supported by well-trained Welsh crossbowmen, whereas the native Irish still used slings and stones for weaponry, and when they did ride horses, rode them bareback."[3]

The outmatched Irish defenders were easily defeated. The Normans had a series of easy victories in the southeastern reaches of Ireland

---

[3] Neville, Peter. *A Traveller's History of Ireland.* 1992.

between the years 1169 and 1171. Of particular significance was the Normans' taking of Dublin in 1170.

At this time, England was ruled by King Henry II, who was a modernizer and sought to pull Britain out of the Dark Ages. King Henry II was also a vigorous champion of expansion. But he had some ulterior motives in doing so.

In 1171, Henry became embroiled in religious controversy after his leading antagonist in regard to the faith—Thomas Becket—was killed. King Henry II and Thomas Becket had once been close friends. The king even appointed Becket as an archbishop. Things did not go quite as planned, however. Becket managed to stoke the king's wrath by vigorously arguing over what the exact relationship should be between the church and state.

The king's relationship with Becket continued to deteriorate. This discord came to a terrifying and violent head in December 1170 when knights loyal to the king burst into Canterbury Cathedral and forcibly laid their hands upon Becket. It has been said that they initially intended to arrest him, but during the course of the struggle, one of the knights sliced off a good portion of the top of Becket's head with their sword. Becket was left to bleed to death in the church. This bloody act generated quite a bit of scandal.

Henry was suspected of having been behind the hit, and he was actually condemned by the church for carrying out the murder. He was told to embark upon a "suitable deed" to vindicate himself, and it seems that the conquest of Ireland was the quest that he settled upon.

However, once Ireland was militarily subdued, Henry proved to be too distracted to adequately administer it. He tried to leave this task to subordinates and ultimately placed his own son, John, in charge in 1177. The only trouble was that his son was only nine at the time! This meant that the true power would lay with those who advised John, and these men often had competing loyalties and motivations.

Nevertheless, in 1185, King Henry went as far as to petition the pope to have John recognized as the king of Ireland. John paid a visit to Ireland in 1185 for the first time and stayed there for several months, observing the antagonism on display between the Norman occupiers and the local Irish leaders. John did not seem to help matters, as his arrogant manners were put on full display before the Irish chieftains. Although this incident is disputed by historians, some accounts claim that he actually pulled on the beards of some of the Irish leaders who came to meet with him. If that story is true, such actions are not endearing, to say the least.

John was more than content to leave the actual rule of Ireland up to others. After King Henry II passed in 1189, the English crown went to John's older brother, Richard the Lionheart. Lionheart was the famed Crusader who led an army to the Middle East and fought Sultan Saladin of Egypt and Syria to a standstill.

Richard would perish in 1199, making his brother John the new king of England, as well as the supposed king of Ireland. It was not until 1210 that good old King John, now all grown up, decided to throw his weight around and enforce his rule over Ireland. This enforced rule meant the establishment of a feudal state within Ireland.

Norman occupation saw Irish land, which had been the domain of the Irish chiefs, be divvied up and handed out to English nobility. This actually created a slight problem for King John down the road when some Anglo-Norman barons began to grow a bit too big for their britches. In 1210, King John made his way to Dublin to put down any potential opposition and make it clear who was calling the shots. Soon, active fighting erupted with these barons, and John's troops besieged the strategic site of Carrickfergus Castle.

This event led the powerful Anglo-Norman baron named Hugh de Lacy to leave Ireland and head to Scotland. Hugh de Lacy had previously been an important figure and was a main participant in the early stages of the Norman invasion of Ireland under John's father, King Henry II. Hugh de Lacy was also an integral part of pacifying the local Irish, a task that was deemed to have been completed by the year 1175. For his efforts, he had been awarded control of most of County Meath. His abrupt departure for Scotland, however, left his Irish land up for grabs.

King John had his own problems in England in the meantime. Due to the discontent of his own nobles at home, he was forced to sign off on the groundbreaking legal document known as the Magna Carta in 1215. This document ensured that the land-owning subjects of the Crown would be granted a fair hearing in court if a dispute erupted. The Magna Carta also ensured that there would be no unwarranted coercion made against them.

The notion that one should be allowed their day in court and should not be attacked for no reason likely seems like common sense to most of us today. However, these were major milestones in Britain at the time. Prior to signing the Magna Carta, kings could basically do whatever they wanted; now, there were at least some safeguards for the nobility (the rest would have to wait).

After this had been achieved, a balance between the Anglo-Norman rulers of Ireland and the king of England was established. The terms of the Magna Carta were meant to apply to Ireland just as much as England, and a later, more specific charter would be issued in 1217 that noticeably substituted "London" for "Dublin." Otherwise, the charter was much the same.

Not long after King John signed the original Magna Carta, he died. He passed away in 1216 and was succeeded by his young son, Henry III.

Both Henry III and his successor, Edward I, were content to rule Ireland from afar through royal officials. They would not pay an official visit to the region during their respective reigns. King Edward, for his part, did make an effort to at least get the Irish on board with English common law.

Edward sent word in 1277 for his plans to incorporate the Irish into the English civil system, but the Irish were content to stick with their own old legal codes and traditions, so they largely ignored him. This was a setback for effective streamlining governance in Ireland. It left Ireland locked out of the integrated circuitry that ran through early English bureaucracy, which was essentially a forerunner to what would become Parliament.

Locked out of the bureaucratic world, Ireland would have to be ruled by the decree of the king of England. Meanwhile, the Irish had kept up their tradition of a high king, even if the position was a rather toothless one. Brian O'Neill of the powerful O'Neill clan became high king in 1258. But if it is any demonstration of how arbitrary the distinction had become, the title was actually offered to Norway's king in 1263 in an abortive attempt to gain Norse support against the English.

Brian O'Neill was defeated by Anglo-Norman colonists and killed in battle in 1260. Traditionally, this would have been the cue for the Irish to begin the long, troubling process of squabbling amongst themselves for a successor. But rather than looking inward, they ultimately looked outward. In 1263, they offered the high kingship of Ireland to King

Haakon IV of Norway.

The fact that the Irish would rather be ruled by a complete outsider in the form of a Norwegian king demonstrates the complete contempt they had for the hated Anglo-Norman landlords and the English king who backed them.

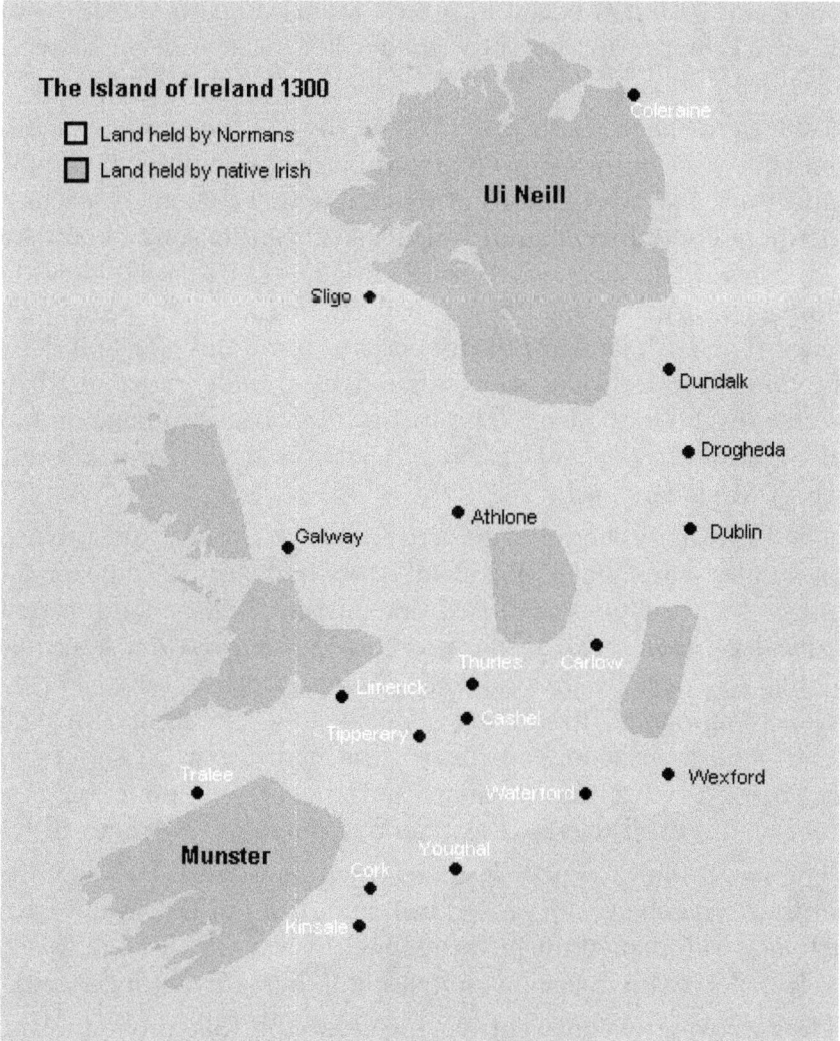

The Island of Ireland 1300

☐ Land held by Normans
☐ Land held by native Irish

Ui Neill

Coleraine
Sligo
Dundalk
Drogheda
Athlone
Galway
Dublin
Thurles    Carlow
Limerick
Cashel
Tipperary
Tralee
Wexford
Waterford
Munster
Youghal
Cork
Kinsale

Ireland in 1300.

Ireland's prosperity would rise and fall during this period. Ireland became a big agricultural producer and also specialized in the export of wool. Irish commodities like these were exported to England and many other localities far and wide. The Anglo-Norman landlords profited from these enterprises, leading to the rise of sturdy stone castles, which dotted the landscape.

However, the Irish grew restless. By the end of King Edward I's reign in 1307, the Irish had begun to protest against English (Anglo-Norman) authority. Edward II, who ruled until 1327, dealt with an increasingly agitated Irish public.

Why were the Irish so upset? Well, by this point in Irish history, about half of all of the Anglo-Norman barons were absentee landlords, meaning that they spent more of their time in England, Normandy, or somewhere else rather than in Ireland. You can imagine the frustration of the native Irish. They were being lorded over by people they viewed as foreign usurpers, and these usurpers did not even remain in the country. The Irish landed nobility perhaps hated this situation the most since they were the ones who suffered the ramifications of what this absenteeism did to the land. The Irish who managed to hang on to their lands faced the specter of very bad neighbors in the form of these lax Anglo-Norman landlords.

The English also began to enforce restrictions against Anglo-Normans who decided to remain in Ireland and went "native," meaning they adopted Irish customs, married into Irish families, and essentially became Irish themselves in the process. England did not want this. Its goal was to Anglicize Ireland and diminish Irish culture. These acts essentially amounted to cultural genocide (the eradication of a whole culture), and their actions might be a bit hard for us to fathom today. Concerns over this fraternization and the feared influence of Irish culture on the English led to the infamous Statutes of Kilkenny in 1366.

The statutes were actually instituted by King Edward III's son, Lionel. The prince marched into Ireland with an army, but he did not have too much luck with martial might at the time. Instead, he decided to achieve what he failed to do in blatant conquest with bureaucratic legislation.

He convened a conference in the town of Kilkenny and laid out statutes to enforce English customs on the Anglo-Irish. Today, we would likely consider these statutes to be blatantly discriminatory against the Irish. The statutes stated that the English were not only to refrain from marrying the Irish but were also to basically minimize all relations with the locals.

It was forbidden to speak the Irish language, and people were not allowed to follow any local rules or customs. Prior to this, the close proximity of Anglo-Irish among the native Irish had created a sense of familiarity; these statutes sought to seed alienation and fan the flames of animosity between them.

Considering previous efforts to better streamline Ireland into Britain, these statutes seem horribly counterproductive. Lionel's statutes were mostly ignored, just as much as his army had been. It was not until a decade later that King Richard II was able to raise a formidable enough body of troops to actually make the statutes the law of the land.

Richard II was deposed in 1399, but the statutes continued to have an effect. By 1450, the only real portion of Ireland that the king of England had real control over was the so-called "English Pale," which consisted of Dublin and some twenty miles of surrounding land. English control over the rest of Ireland remained aspirational at best.

# Chapter 5: Tudors and Plantations

*"I find that I sent wolves not shepherds to govern Ireland, for they have left me nothing but ashes and carcasses to reign over!"*

*-Queen Elizabeth I*

Of all of the outside forces that threatened to dominate Ireland, the most formidable would prove to be England's Tudor dynasty. The Tudor dynasty, kicked off by Henry VII in 1485, would begin a renewed interest on the part of the English in bringing Ireland to heel. In total, the Tudors would wage a succession of four all-out wars to bring Ireland fully into its sphere of influence. But before we get into all of that, it would be a good idea to understand a bit of the background of the Tudor dynasty itself.

It all began back in 1483 when England's King Edward IV perished. Richard of Gloucester momentarily seized power after deposing Edward's twelve-year-old son, who was also named Edward. Richard was successfully challenged in 1485 by a rich nobleman named Henry Tudor. Henry was able to raise an army and put an end to Richard's reign, securing the throne for himself. Henry Tudor then became known as Henry VII.

King Henry VII did not have much of an impact on Ireland, but his successor, King Henry VIII, most certainly would. King Henry VIII tried to fully enforce and greatly expand upon the aforementioned Statutes of Kilkenny.

So, who exactly was this overbearing Henry VIII? In order to understand his policies, we must understand the man. Henry VIII was coronated on June 24th, 1509. His forebearer, although an able steward in many ways as it pertained to domestic policies, was not the most charming and rarely engaged the public. However, his flamboyant successor, Henry VIII, was different. He was determined to make a big show of things from the very start.

On his very coronation day, he made sure to create an extravagant display that would capture the public's imagination. He also punished his father's harshest taskmasters—Richard Empson and Edmund Dudley—to the utter delight of British subjects everywhere.

However, all was not well in the household of Henry VIII due to the fact that his wife Catherine seemed entirely unable to produce a son. Having a male heir was considered vital to the British throne in those days, so this was no small matter. Henry VIII agonized over this problem until he finally decided that he would have to put his wife away and find a new one who was capable of producing baby boys.

But how to dismiss Catherine and stay within the bounds of Catholic teaching? That was Henry's number one objective.

He thought about it for some time and seemed to find a unique solution. His eyes sighted the Bible verse Leviticus 20:21, which states, "If a man shall take his brother's wife, it is an impunity: he hath uncovered his brother's nakedness: they shall be childless." For Henry VIII, this verse seemed to give him a reason to put away his wife and an explanation for the state that they were in.

Catherine had been married to Henry's older brother, Arthur, but he perished shortly after they wed. Henry then took it upon himself to marry the widowed Catherine. However, Henry began to think the marriage was cursed because Catherine was unable to give him a son. Catherine did give birth to a daughter, Mary, but having a woman take the throne of England was unheard of at that time.

Henry believed he was within the bounds of scripture to set Catherine aside and that it was the only right thing to do. Indicating that his marriage was a mistake, he sought an annulment to correct the perceived error. He petitioned Pope Clement VIII to oblige him, but the pope was not willing.

This makes sense, though. The pope was torn between his desire to please the king of England, who had been a loyal ally, and Holy Roman Emperor Charles V, who also just so happened to be Catherine of Aragon's nephew. The pope did not wish to alienate either one, so he mostly put off making a decision. Henry ultimately lost his patience with the Catholic Church and sought a unilateral annulment before breaking with the church completely.

Henry issued the Act of Supremacy in 1534, which made him the head of the Church of England. The English monarch would now reign over the state and also the state's religion.

Henry would go on to marry Anne Boleyn, but after she was unable to produce a son, he had her executed in 1536. He then married Jane Seymour. She would produce a male heir, the future King Edward VI, but she perished in 1537, leading Henry to marry Anne of Cleves.

Henry was an obstinate character as it pertained to wives at this point in his life. Upon the first sign of frustration, he had his latest marriage with Anne of Cleves annulled (at least she was able to live in comfort and not face the executioner!). Henry wed Catherine Howard, who lost her head in 1542. That marriage was followed by his marriage to Catherine Parr, his last and final wife, who would remain with Henry until he perished in 1547.

Now that we have covered the infamous backstory of Henry VIII and his many unfortunate wives, we can rewind the narrative a bit to see how this notorious king related to Irish history. The stakes in Ireland were significantly raised just a few years after Henry came to the throne. In 1513, a momentous seat change occurred when Gearóid Óg, also known as Gerald FitzGerald, became the ninth earl of Kildare.

Many are likely not familiar with Gearóid Óg or Kildare, but he and the region he ruled are immensely important. Kildare was a region that bordered the ever-shrinking Anglo-Irish enclave in Dublin known as the Pale. Considered a strategic frontier, it was ruled by warlord-like earls who served as de facto kings of Ireland. King Henry did not like how Gearóid was getting on, and in 1519, Henry ordered him to report to London.

After Gearóid Óg reported to the English monarch, King Henry was not too terribly impressed. By the following year, in May of 1520, he managed to get Gearóid Óg dismissed in favor of Thomas Howard as Lord Deputy. Howard, who was the uncle of both Anne Boleyn and Catherine Howard, immediately began to try his hand at crushing the martial might of rebels in Leinster, Ulster, and the Midlands.

He stood against the powerful O'Neill family. Thomas Howard did not last long and was soon recalled to take part in conflicts against the

French. Between 1522 and 1529, there were several dismissals and recalls, with no appointed deputy lasting longer than a couple of years.

After Henry broke with the Catholic Church, all hell broke loose. When Henry issued the Act of Supremacy in 1534, the earl of Kildare, Thomas FitzGerald, known as "Silken Thomas" because of his penchant for fine silk, stood up against Henry, roundly denouncing him as a heretic. The Irish were staunch Catholics, and as such, Silken Thomas was seen as a populist Catholic leader of sorts by the Irish people. Not only that, but he also positioned himself as a potential tool for both the pope and the Holy Roman emperor.

To have such a terrible thorn emerge in his side was an intolerable nuisance for King Henry VIII, and he immediately took action. King Henry VIII sent some 2,300 troops to Ireland, led by Sir William Skeffington. Henry tasked the men with pacifying Kildare.

This group of troops besieged the formidable Maynooth Castle in March 1535. The castle fell, and on March 25th, the English troops wreaked their vengeance on twenty-five prisoners of war who had their heads chopped off outside the toppled fortress walls. Thomas FitzGerald was executed, along with many of his relatives. This was the end of Kildare's power, and the earldom was officially dismantled in 1537.

Since the de facto rule of Kildare was no more, this meant that King Henry VIII would have to take a more direct role in Ireland from here on out. So, he installed a thoroughly English governor, who was backed up by a formidable English garrison of troops. Henry's dominance was made official in 1541 when he was proclaimed "Lord of Ireland."

The previous Irish power players were forced to show their allegiance to Henry. Those who were loyal to the English Crown were made liege lords and given the distinction of being made earls of their domain. Of course, not everyone readily agreed to this. Some decided to defy the ambitions of the English king. These dissenters—at least in King Henry's eyes—were nothing more than rogues and rebels.

One of the most prominent among them was an Irish chieftain named Dubhdara O'Malley. O'Malley had a great fleet of ships, which he made good use of by speedily sailing from one place to another. O'Malley's fleet was even known to sail as far as sympathetic Catholic Spain. To the Irish, O'Malley was a freedom fighter, but to the English, he was a pirate.

However, it was his daughter Grace who would go down in infamy for her stunning raids on English property. They were so stunning that she would be forever be dubbed "Grace O'Malley, the Pirate Queen." Grace began her career early, allegedly sneaking onto one of her dad's ships and pretending to be a cabin boy. Grace grew up, got married to a prominent Irishman named Donal O'Flaherty, and raised a family before she rose to prominence and became a great thorn in England's side.

She and her crew mostly raided merchant ships. Upon boarding the craft, Grace and her followers often demanded the percentage of the value of the goods that the merchant craft carried. If the besieged merchants could not pay up, these pirates simply seized the goods themselves. It may sound terrible that the Irish would ever resort to piracy, but we cannot forget that piracy had been a long-established practice in Ireland. Additionally, King Henry VIII first decided to pick sides, so it is not all that surprising that some of the Irish would "go rogue" and utilize underhanded tactics, such as piracy, in a bid to strike back.

King Henry VIII would perish in 1547 after much of this damage to Ireland had already been done. And what damage are we speaking of? Well, besides usurping ancestral titles from the local Irish, Henry essentially sowed enmity between the local families who bowed to the Crown and those who refused. He also instituted many of the conditions that would lead to unrest and even outright famine in the future.

Henry's immediate successors would begin the colonization process of Ireland through a series of plantations. Henry was initially succeeded by his son, Edward VI. He would only live to be fifteen, and the biggest impact he made during his short tenure was his implementation of the *Book of Common Prayer* to Ireland. It was the first printed book in Ireland that was in English. This was done, of course, under the heavy influence of Edward's Protestant handlers, who wished to convert Irish Catholics to their way of thinking.

Proving how easily the winds of fate could shift, the Protestant-friendly boy king would perish (as would all of Henry's dreams of a long-lived male heir), and Henry's daughter Mary—a diehard Catholic—became queen. She was known as "Bloody Mary" because of her vengeful nature and her bloody reversal of many Protestant policies, which led to hundreds being executed on religious grounds. But despite her penchant for Catholicism, Mary had no patience for a rebellious Ireland. She sought to pacify the Irish by installing plantations in the counties of Laois and Offaly in Ireland in the 1550s. These plantations were supposed to set an "English example," which favored pastoral farming above anything else.

However, the harsh Queen Mary's reign was just about as brief as her ill-fated predecessor. Mary passed away in 1558, opening the door for Queen Elizabeth to take the throne.

Queen Elizabeth continued the trend of Ireland's colonization by way of plantations. Queen Elizabeth also returned to the Protestant-friendly policies of Edward, which was a great boon to the Protestant minority in Ireland at the time.

But Queen Elizabeth would face a long spate of unrest, which had its roots in the 1559 election of Shane O'Neill as the earl of Tyrone. Shane was the son of the former earl, Conn Bacagh O'Neill. According to Gaelic custom, Shane was the rightful heir. However, the English government in Ireland, headed by Thomas Radclyffe, Earl of Sussex, did not recognize this claim and instead favored his cousin, Brian. The Irish recognized Shane, and he soon brought all of his rivals under his control. He did so by diplomacy when he could, but he did use force when necessary.

Thomas Radclyffe's government in Sussex did not take too kindly to all of this and viewed Shane as an ominous threat to English interests in the region. Fighting ensued, and in 1562, Shane O'Neill was forced to come to London to give an account of his actions. It is said that he begged the queen for mercy and swore that he would, from that point forward, be her loyal servant.

It seems Queen Elizabeth did indeed offer her mercy, as she agreed to recognize Shane as the Earl of Tyrone. By 1564, however, these plans had once again broken down, and Shane again began to launch rebellions against the English. He invaded the Pale and razed Armagh to the ground in 1566. He also drove into Ulster, where he viciously assaulted the Scottish MacDonnells, who had their stronghold there. During this period, Ulster was a hotbed of plantation activity.

Shane was brought to heel in 1567 when he was trounced by the forces of Hugh O'Donnell. But although his rebellion was shattered, O'Neill himself managed to escape.

After he tried to negotiate with the Scots, he met his end. The Scots were actively collaborating with the English at the time and decided it would better serve their interests to have Shane killed. He was summarily executed, and his decapitated head was promptly shipped off to the queen's Lord Deputy, Sir Henry Sidney. Upon receipt of the head, the queen knew that the threat of Shane O'Neill, the former earl of Tyrone, was finally at an end.

However, soon after this revolt against English encroachment was snuffed out, another conflagration erupted in the form of the so-called "Geraldine Revolt." The revolt is also known as the Desmond Rebellions. This tumult is centered around the FitzGerald family (also referred to as the Geraldines), who controlled Desmond, and their struggle with England. This revolt broke out in 1569 and would last all the way until 1583.

This revolt had two driving forces. First of all, it was sparked by mere jealousy between the Geraldines and the highly influential earl of Ormond, Thomas Butler. It was also due to the hostility that had arisen in regard to the relations of now mostly Protestant England and strongly Catholic Spain.

King Philip II was the king of Spain at the time and had long desired to bring England back to the Catholic fold. Queen Elizabeth had become something of a Protestant champion. England would defend—or at least lend support—to Protestant territories that Spain was at war with, such as the Netherlands. The Irish Catholics wished to link up with Spain as a means to offset their English opponents.

These two driving forces would lead to even more forceful resistance to the English plantation scheme in Ireland. Leading the revolt was James FitzMaurice FitzGerald, who was the cousin of the fifteenth earl of Desmond. FitzMaurice sought to gain international support for a stand against the English.

He was not quite successful, as he did not gain military support from the French or Spanish, but he did manage to gain support from Pope Pius V, who went as far as to have Queen Elizabeth excommunicated. Since Henry VIII had severed England from the dictates of Rome, such things had very little meaning. For the Protestants of England—many of whom viewed the pope as an insufferable tyrant—excommunication could be worn as a badge of honor rather than a sign of disgrace.

In July 1579, FitzMaurice took an army and sent it to smash into the English forces. However, FitzMaurice, for all of his bravery and determination, would perish before he reached his destination.

Was he killed by forces loyal to Queen Elizabeth? Not exactly. FitzMaurice was killed in what seems to be an entirely unrelated scuffle with one of his cousins, Theobald Burke, and his minions.

Although this ambush was unexpected, the accounts of FitzMaurice's last stand are rather riveting. It has been said that he was shot in the chest, and the wound proved to be fatal. But just prior to succumbing to his injuries, the infuriated FitzMaurice used his sword to hack through Theobald's men until he reached his cousin Theobald himself.

In his fury, FitzMaurice managed to kill Theobald on the spot, running him through with his sword. This would be the last act of the mighty FitzMaurice, as he collapsed and died of his injuries shortly afterward. FitzMaurice stands out as one of the greats of Irish resistance to outside oppression, yet ironically enough, he perished as a victim of Irish infighting.

At any rate, the revolt would peter out a few years later, coming to a close in 1583.

One fearsome former rebel who had become quite weary of all of the fighting at this point was the aforementioned "Pirate Queen," Grace O'Malley. O'Malley was now in her later years and a widow. She was worried about the future of the next generation. Her fears and insecurity led her to break down and write a letter directly to Queen Elizabeth herself.

The letter was written sometime in 1593 and would lead to one of the most epic moments in English and Irish history. Grace O'Malley and Queen Elizabeth actually met in person to discuss the latest turmoil in Ireland. Grace and Queen Elizabeth had several sit-down conversations between June and September of 1593. Much of what they discussed lies in the realm of folklore, but some believe that Elizabeth attempted to offer Grace a title, which Grace refused.

More fighting would erupt in 1594 when an English supply convoy was assaulted by Irish rebels. Some fifty-six English troops were killed in the attack. This marked the start of the Nine Years' War.

Leading the charge against the English during this conflict was a powerful earl of Tyrone named Hugh O'Neill. And yes, he was related to the previous rebel Shane O'Neill. However, Hugh led a very different life than his ill-fated relative. Hugh actually spent much of his early years in England, whereas Shane is said to have never spoken a word of English in his life. Hugh was also a Protestant, whereas Shane O'Neill had been a Catholic through and through.

Hugh, who was considered a friend of Queen Elizabeth, was initially considered a valuable pawn to be used in Irish affairs. When he returned to Ireland to stake his ancestral claim, he was being groomed to be an agent of the English. However, in 1598, he decided to join the ongoing rebellion. That year, he handily defeated an English army at the Battle of Yellow Ford near Armagh.

Queen Elizabeth was greatly disturbed to hear of these tidings and immediately dispatched the earl of Essex to see what was afoot. This ill-fated earl quite literally lost his head and was succeeded by Lord Charles Blount, 8th Baron of Mountjoy, who was deputized to take on the Irish.

Charles Blount went down in infamy for his take-no-prisoners approach and scorched-earth tactics. In his struggle against the Irish rebels, he not only killed people, including men, women, and children, but also their livestock. He butchered cattle in the fields and then made sure to burn down any crops growing on Irish farms. Actions such as these would lead to a "manmade" famine. Countless would perish, and the devastation unleashed in the early 1600s would set the template for future scourges.

Interestingly, the most shocking episode as it pertains to Mountjoy's scorched-earth campaign came from his own personal secretary, Fynes Moryson, who recalled a terrible scene around the Irish town of Newry. According to Moryson, children were seen roasting and eating the flesh of their dead mother. Moryson claims that when these kids were asked why they were doing such a terrible thing, they answered they could not get any other meat. When asked what happened to their cattle, the children matter-of-factly reported, "The Englishmen had taken them away."

It is easy to assume that this account is either false or grossly exaggerated, but since it came from Mountjoy's own secretary, one has to wonder what purpose such a tall tale would serve. Did Mountjoy encourage his secretary to produce these tales because they made him look good? Did he promote these stories because he wanted to shock the Irish? Was he proud to have starved the Irish to cannibalism? Or was the account—as shocking as it is—true? Historians may be divided on this particular point, but the well-documented famines that struck the land are not open for debate.

Queen Elizabeth died in March 1603, with much of the plantation system still very much in flux. Just a few days after her passing, the Nine Years War came to a close with the signing of the Treaty of Mellifont, which granted some religious concessions to Catholics and recognized Hugh O'Neill's and his family's titles and lands in exchange for Hugh and his followers to respect and accept English authority. Interestingly, the Pirate Queen, Grace O'Malley, perished that same year.

The most immediate aftereffect of the Nine Years' War was that many leading figures in previous rebellious strongholds, such as Munster and Ulster, were missing in action. For instance, on September 4th, 1607, Hugh O'Neill, Earl of Tyrone, as well as Rory O'Donnell, Earl of Tyrconnell, the younger brother of Hugh O'Donnell, hopped on a French freighter and left all of their holdings behind.

Apparently unwilling to withstand the increasing pressure on their domain and perhaps hoping to seek support abroad, they fled to continental Europe. This event was known as "the Flight of the Earls," and it, more than anything else, marked the beginning of a massive rush by the English to claim vacated Irish land. It did not take long for the English to lay claim to the various Irish estates that were up for grabs once the Irish elite had left.

Even though both men—O'Neill and O'Donnell—would ultimately perish as exiles in Rome, their former lands, as well as other confiscated properties, would be the home of brand-new plantations. Large swathes of northern and southern Ireland were open for English settlers willing to stake a claim.

In 1610, new rules were enacted that showed England's true goal: to have English residents outpace the local Irish. King James I and his court hammered out new protocols on how to handle these plantations. The new rules were called Conditions of the Plantation of Ulster.

Although the wording of these new rules mentioned only Ulster, the new laws also applied to Donegal, Tyrone, Derry, Armagh, Fermanagh, and Cavan. A big part of the new measures involved the concerted effort to make the implantation of English "cultural values" among the native Irish who remained a routine practice. This was perhaps most evident in Derry, where the English thrust was so pronounced that the name was actually changed to "Londonderry" since Londoners were so involved in its transformation. Such things are almost insulting to residents of Derry today, who likely cringe whenever they hear the Anglicized version of their town's name. But as writer and historian John Gibney rightly described it, these undertakings were a case of "social engineering on a massive scale."[4]

King James seized prime real estate in the Ulster counties of Tyrone, Fermanagh, Donegal, Coleraine, Cavan, and Armagh. This land was then sold on the cheap to British settlers who were willing to make the move. Initially, many of these new landlords tried to recruit fellow Protestants to work their estates, but they quickly realized it would be cheaper and more practical to simply hire the local Catholics who were already there.

However, it was not all bad for the Irish—that is to say, the poor Irish, who did not have much to lose in the first place. Some economic gains were made after 1603 from which the poorer classes of Irish benefited. From the signing of the Treaty of Mellifont all the way to the mid-17th century, great gains were made in textile production and shipbuilding. All of these enterprises resulted in additional new jobs for the lower-class Irish. Shipbuilding, unfortunately, ended up having negative consequences, as it resulted in the rapid deforestation of large sections of Ireland, leading to timber shortages all throughout the 1630s.

The 1630s is an important marker of progress as it pertains to the English plantations in Ireland. According to writer, historian, and Irish guru John Gibney, by this decade, "the new British presence in Ireland was firmly ensconced."[5] The contentious makeup that would long haunt the region had truly taken shape. Rich Protestant landlords literally lorded over the poor Catholics, creating a simmering cauldron of discontent.

It is true that the poor Irish had jobs, laboring away for these affluent transplants, but their own culture was being oppressed at every turn. Yes, it could be said that by this point, Ireland had already been utterly and irrevocably changed. Little did anyone know, however, that the worst was yet to come.

---

[4] Gibney, John. *A Short History of Ireland: 1500-2000.* 2017.
[5] Gibney, John. *A Short History of Ireland: 1500-2000.* 2017.

# Chapter 6: The Great Famine and Its Consequences

*"Why should Ireland be treated as a geographical fragment of England—Ireland is not a geographical fragment, but a nation."*

*-Charles Stewart Parnell*

Life in Ireland had never been easy, but by the 1630s, conditions had become considerably worse. These dire straits would lead to mass migrations. Some Irish would try their luck in continental Europe, but others would find a new escape valve by way of a continent across the Atlantic called North America.

Irish migration to North America can be tracked in several waves, from the 1630s all the way to the great migrations of the 1840s. The Irish presence was well established in North America by the time of the American Revolution of 1775, and perhaps no one supported the establishment of a free and independent United States more than the Irish. This makes sense. Why wouldn't the Irish be eager to support the independence of a land that would win them a secure refuge and be entirely free from the meddling of the British Crown?

The Irish numbered around half a million at the time of the American War of Independence, and a huge percentage of their number fought to free the nascent United States from Britain's grip. After the American Revolutionary War came to a close, the British were aware they had an increasing problem with the Irish, both abroad and at home.

In an attempt to placate the increasingly distressed Irish, as well as to consolidate British authority, the Acts of Union were promoted in 1800. This act established what would be called the United Kingdom of Great Britain.

For those who are unaware, the term "Great Britain" refers to the greater island of Britain, which includes Scotland, Wales, and England. Ireland was lumped in with these three nations to create what was termed a "United Kingdom." Today, the United Kingdom still exists, but it only retains the northernmost portion of Ireland, known, aptly enough, as Northern Ireland. However, back in the year 1800, the Acts of Union included all of Ireland.

The Acts of Union were a complete slap in the face for many Irish since it disbanded the Parliament of Ireland, which had been hosted in Dublin, in favor of Irish representatives making their way to Westminster, England, instead. Others pointed out that not having their own separate institutions was a step toward better equality.

It was also argued that Irish Protestants would benefit because instead of being a minority in what was still a largely Catholic Ireland, they could become part of the majority of this newly united kingdom. They would be a supermajority of Protestants, as it were, since they were being lumped in with all of the other Protestants in England and other parts of the realm. However, many Irish Protestants felt a great deal of resentment at having this new arrangement foisted upon them.

One can only imagine just how disenfranchised the Irish Catholics must have felt. The notion that their homeland was included in a political union from which they themselves were mostly excluded certainly could not have produced any fans of the British Crown. This perceived exclusion would sow the seeds for further violence.

Now, the favored minority of Protestant Ireland, which, in itself, was largely the scions of the plantation era, had to look increasingly to London for support, whereas the excluded Irish Catholics found even more reasons to look away.

The Irish Protestants felt rightfully threatened by the growing animosity of their less fortunate Catholic neighbors. This insecurity led to the formation of the Orange Order, a fraternal organization said to be loosely patterned off of the Freemasons. The Orange Order focused on the brotherhood of Protestants in what Irish historian Paul F. State describes as being "a sectarian alliance that espoused fierce defense of the union."[6] By the 1820s, the Orange Order and their fanatic loyalty to the Union Jack had reached its height.

While the Irish Protestant, land-holding minority rallied around the flag (at least for the most part), the Catholic majority, which comprised some 80 percent of Ireland's population at the time, created their own underground associations. Members of these groups were known as Ribbonmen, and their organizations had names such as Sons of the Shamrock, Society of St. Patrick, and Patriotic Association of the Shamrock. These groups openly antagonized the Orange Order and often spoke of their desire to spill "Orange blood."

Despite the bold threats, the Irish Catholics remained disenfranchised. However, there was a somewhat successful political organization started by an Irish Catholic lawyer by the name of Daniel O'Connell. O'Connell wanted Catholic emancipation. He founded the Catholic Association in 1823 to help him meet his goal.

Portrait of Daniel O'Connell.
https://commons.wikimedia.org/wiki/File:Daniel_O%27Connell_-_Project_Gutenberg_13103.jpg

Daniel O'Connell's Catholic Association sought to make use of the global ties that linked Ireland to the seat of the Catholic Church in Rome, as well as capitalize on inroads made in Ireland through the Irish

---

[6] State, F. Paul. A Brief History of Ireland. 2009.

enclaves that linked Irish commerce. O'Connell and his Catholic Association faced pushback, but beyond all odds, he managed to rise above adversity in a tremendous way. He was even elected as a member of Parliament in 1828, representing County Clare.

This was a watershed moment for Irish Catholics everywhere, but even so, most were not faring so well. Many had become farmhands who eked out a living as tenant farmers. They were given a couple of acres, a cabin, perhaps a cow, and a field to grow potatoes, which had become an Irish staple.

By 1830, the potato had become the main source of nourishment for many Irish. The potato replaced fish and even milk, both of which had previously been the bounty of Irish fishermen and dairy farmers. The Irish were relegated to small plots of land, so they grew the potato out of convenience and necessity. Potatoes are a hardy crop that can be grown on small-scale farms, and potatoes are able to provide ample nutrients.

The Irish climate and especially its soil, which leans toward being a bit on the acidic side, proved to be quite conducive for growing this particular crop in the 1800s. However, there were two major problems. Potatoes cannot be stored for prolonged periods of time, and they are susceptible to disease. In the summer of 1845—the fateful year of the first widespread potato famine in Ireland—it seemed that the elements were conspiring to ruin that year's potato crops.

In consideration of the fact that many Irish victims of the potato famine ended up fleeing to the United States, it is with some irony to note that the cause of the Irish potato famine is said to have originated in the United States. It is believed that a rare fungus came from North America and spread, affecting the potato crops in Britain by quickly decimating all of the potatoes it came in contact with. The blighted potatoes were first witnessed in England before the blight spread to Ireland.

The fungus turned leaves and stalks into blackened, crumbly dust. Potato farmers in Ireland tried their best to salvage crops by removing the affected parts of the plant, but they soon learned that if the leaves were black, the potatoes were likely already affected. According to one account, which appeared in a periodical of the day called the *Freeman's Journal*, a farmer had been harvesting a bountiful crop of perfect, healthy potatoes one day, only to find the rest rendered into "filthy, odorous black mush" the next.

Thomas Gallagher famously wrote about the famine in his book *Paddy's Lament.* He described a "sulphureous, sewerlike" odor, which was "carried by the wind from the rotting plants in the first-struck places." Gallagher furthermore asserted that "Farmers who had gone to bed imbued with the image of their lush potato gardens were awakened by this awful smell and by the dogs howling their disapproval of it."

No matter how hungry the Irish might have been, they were not going to scoop up the nasty, mushy, smelly remnants of what used to be a potato and eat it. Thanks to a pesky fungus now known as *Phytophthora infestans*, their potato crop was destroyed. But what exactly were they to do? Without the potatoes, their main source of nourishment was gone.

The suffering was as much psychological as it was physical. As one member of the local clergy who chronicled this suffering stated, "In many places, the wretched people were seated on the fences of their decaying gardens wringing their hands and wailing bitterly the destruction that had left them foodless."[7]

One can only imagine how devastating all of this must have been. For those who staked just about everything on this crop, it must have seemed like the world had come to an end. Many with a more superstitious bent likely associated the famine with some sort of impending Armageddon. Even though the potato famine did not turn out to be a harbinger of a global doomsday, it sure was hell for the Irish.

It is said that the starving masses did their best to survive. Some learned how to improvise by foraging, hunting wild game, and fishing. These means of food acquisition were rife with difficulty and danger for those who were inexperienced in the practice. For example, people who did not know what they were doing could very easily devour poisonous plants or eat diseased meat in their desperate scramble to find sustenance. According to some accounts, there were even instances of cannibalism reported in the counties of Cork, Kerry, Mayo, and Galway.

Many historical narratives give the impression that the British government did nothing to try and help the starving Irish, but this is not true. It could be easily argued that the British officials did not do enough, but it would be inaccurate to say that they did nothing at all.

---

[7] Neville, Peter. *A Traveller's History of Ireland.* 1992.

The British government, under the administration of Prime Minister Robert Peel, was blindsided by the potato blight. It was certainly an unexpected event, and as such, the first order of business for Peel's government was to figure out what had happened. Many cynical and perhaps even prejudiced members of the British government initially wondered about the veracity of all of the Irish woes they were hearing about. The British were fairly far removed from what was going on in Ireland, and it is also worth noting that the British relied on more than one crop for sustenance. So, for them, the notion that the failure of one crop—the potato—could cause such an outbreak of famine among the Irish seemed hard to believe.

Peter Neville, who wrote *A Traveller's History of Ireland*, was quick to point out that the member of Peel's government put in charge of Irish famine relief, Charles Edward Trevelyan, had made prejudicial statements against the Irish, which, according to Neville, seemed to "have a touch of racism about them."[8]

One of Trevelyan's worst remarks was when he declared that "Ireland must be left to the operation of natural causes," as if it were completely natural for all of the Irish to starve to death. Trevelyan did not view the Irish as proper British subjects in need of help but rather as some sort of second-class citizens who deserved their lot in life. He was of the opinion that the famine needed to run its course. There would be no sympathy from him, only absurd theorizing and ice-cold cynicism.

Many others shared the same views as Charles Edward Trevelyan. They simply refused to believe what was happening. Ireland was part of the greatest empire in the world. The more cynically minded wondered if the Irish were somehow exaggerating their plight. There was certainly a temptation to view the Irish as lazy and inept and that they had brought unnecessary problems on themselves and, by extension, the British government.

Peel instituted a fact-finding commission to make an inquiry into the problem. However, this "scientific inquiry" fell far short of science when they began advising the Irish to do ridiculous things, such as punch holes into the ground near their crops in order to "air them out." Airing out fungus-infested potatoes would not do any good.

---

[8] Neville, Peter. *A Traveller's History of Ireland.* 1992.

When it was realized that the Irish were not exaggerating their issues and that the problem was not going to be fixed easily, efforts were made to somehow help those who had lost their crops.

But despite their hardship, Peel was not into free handouts. In fact, Peel wanted them to work! The Peel government sought to alleviate those hit the hardest by putting them into government-sanctioned workhouses, where the Irish were made to work for their food in terrible conditions.

The workhouses were awful, but for someone starving, it was likely better than nothing. But as the crops continued to fail and the Irish continued to seek relief, it was clear that there simply was not enough room in the workhouses for all of those in need of help.

Fearing that the whole system of relief would collapse, British administrators bought surplus corn from the United States in an effort to provide some form of sustenance to the starving Irish. The government also set up a relief commission to better streamline the doling out of aid.

Most of the Irish had never even seen corn, let alone eaten it. The foodstuff was sold as cornmeal, and many Irish mills were not even equipped to make it. There was a lot of confusion about the new crop, but the Irish took what they could to survive.

Along with corn, money was allocated for a relief fund. Queen Victoria was a generous giver to this relief fund. Of course, the more cynical would rightly point out that she was the queen. If the queen of England could not raise money for the suffering Irish, who were members of the British Empire, then who could?

Interestingly, during this period, the famed American abolitionist Frederick Douglass paid a visit to Ireland. He was absolutely shocked at what he saw. He even informed his compatriot and abolitionist peer William Loyd Garrison that the suffering of the Irish was beyond belief.

Many international charities attempted to help the Irish. One of the famous relief efforts came from the Choctaw tribe in the United States. Having heard of the plight, the Choctaw raised money and sent over five thousand dollars in today's money to the Irish.

Although the Irish suffered greatly, the initial efforts made by the British government to stave off calamity were marginally successful. It might have seemed that Britain had dodged a bullet. However, the famine was not over yet. And when the potato-ravaging fungus returned in 1846, matters became much worse. This time around, the destruction of potato farms was even more widespread.

It seems that the first round of the blight had left spores on the ground, which, due to a wet and rainy season, were submerged deep in the soil. These spores developed a lethal strain of fungus that would overwhelm all of Ireland's potato crops.

Perhaps even worse for the Irish was the fact that the previous prime minister, Robert Peel, and his Tories had been dismissed. The Whigs led by Lord John Russell had taken over the administration.

Russell seemed to lack an understanding of how to deal with the growing crisis and mostly tried a hands-off approach, insisting that local organizations in Ireland should handle the problem. This was no help at all. The British government declared the famine was over in 1847, but the Irish felt the effects of the famine well into 1852.

Many Irish felt they had no choice but to leave their country or starve to death. A mass migration began. Just prior to the famine, Ireland had a population of around eight million. It has been estimated that approximately one million died during the famine. Another million left the country, meaning Ireland lost a quarter of its population in about six years. Irish from all corners of the country made their way to Dublin and other port cities and left on whatever ships they could find with whatever belongings they could carry.

The odds of survival on some of these ships were quite low. The ships became known as "coffin ships." During one voyage to Canada, hundreds perished.

Nevertheless, the Irish continued to flee, with over two million fleeing the country in total. Many headed to Canada or the United States. This number of migrants constituted a stunning quarter of the whole population of Ireland at the time.

The Irish potato famine not only killed a sizeable fraction of the Irish population and led to massive migration abroad, but it also crystallized a strong sense of renewed nationalism among many of the Irish. The Irish who survived this turmoil were hardened and more determined than ever before to rise up and stand for their rights.

# Chapter 7: The Easter Rising: The Birth of Republicanism

*"We don't believe that winning elections and winning any amount of votes will win freedom in Ireland. At the end of the day, it will be the cutting edge of the IRA which will bring freedom."*

*-Martin McGuinness*

After the incredibly devastating potato famine, those who remained in Ireland began to seriously consider independence. It was clear that the British administration was not working, and for many, the potato famine was literally a do-or-die moment. So, the Irish called upon the greatness of their ancestors and tried to martial their warrior spirit to fix their plight.

In 1858, Irish political activist James Stephens launched the Fenian movement. This political movement was named after the Irish soldiers of the past, the Fianna. As historian Paul F. State puts it, "A secret fraternal society, the Fenians (the name alludes to the Fianna army of ancient Irish mythology), was founded in Dublin in March 1858 and in New York City in April 1859, although it may have had informal beginnings a decade earlier in Ireland."[9]

It was not long before this militant group took action. In 1867, matters came to a head when high-ranking members of the Fenian

---

[9] State, F. Paul. A Brief History of Ireland. 2009.

movement were executed after some of their members launched an assault on the police.

The following year, Britain elected a Liberal prime minister, William E. Gladstone. Prime Minister Gladstone would be important in the events of Irish independence. Although he could not quite be characterized as being sympathetic with all of the ambitions of the Irish, he was pragmatic enough to understand an untenable situation when he saw one. Prime Minister Gladstone made some of the first major moves to actually do something about the Irish.

The idea of home rule began to be discussed more and more. The notion of home rule was not calling for a complete break from the British Empire or the United Kingdom; instead, the people who were part of the Home Rule movement wanted the establishment of a separate parliament in Ireland so the Irish could have some say in how their affairs were governed.

Essentially, instead of having every rule dictated to them from London, England, Home Rule advocates were demanding that rulings be made in Dublin, Ireland. All rulings would still have to be approved by higher authorities in the United Kingdom, but direct representation from Ireland would be an integral part of the process.

This was especially important for the landed elite of Ireland since they were the ones who often had to carry the heavy burden of dealing with the poor, starving masses during the potato famine. Many of the better-off Irish landlords had been placed in a truly unenviable position since they were expected to cobble together charitable efforts on the ground without enough help from the politicians in London. Such things served as a glaring indication that Ireland needed some sense of home rule in order to be able to handle some of their problems on their own.

Whether they admitted it or not, there were many in London who could not help but agree due to the mismanagement disaster that had occurred during the potato famine. Not all would openly admit that out loud, of course, out of fear of alienating their English constituents, but they likely saw the writing on the wall all the same.

Under the administration of Prime Minister William Gladstone, the British Parliament implemented the Land Act on August 1st, 1870. This bit of legislation is considered to be the first effort by the British government to truly address the plight of tenant farmers in Ireland.

Seeking to unwind some of the restrictions that had chained the Irish to the land on which they worked, the Land Act gave them basic rights and also promised to hold the landlords accountable if they suddenly decided to evict their tenants for no good reason.

That same year, an Irish politician named Isaac Butt began to advance the cause of home rule and the call for Ireland to have its own separate parliament. Butt's group became known as the Home Rule League, which managed to pick up several seats in the 1874 general election.

These efforts sought to achieve through legislation what countless Irish warlords could never do by force—they sought to bring some sense of homegrown authority back to the Irish homeland.

The Irish found an unlikely champion in Charles Stewart Parnell. Parnell was a land-holding Irish Protestant, but he had his reasons for struggling for the cause of home rule. Parnell's Home Rule Party (also referred to as the Home Rule League) consisted primarily of the tenant farmers who had lost so much during the potato famine. Parnell and his championship of home rule coincided with the rise of the aforementioned Prime Minister William Gladstone.

Gladstone was a liberal politician who took a much more conciliatory position on Ireland than many of his peers at the time. Gladstone made several efforts to push through legislation that would allow Ireland to have greater autonomy. However, these efforts, which were highly unpopular in England, continued to fail.

Even so, the Liberals found themselves in a box. They could not get a majority to support the agenda of home rule, but they also could not afford to lose the sizeable fraction of Irish members of Parliament who supported it.

The conservatives in Britain found it profitable at the ballot box to swing in the complete opposite direction, so Britain became split between one side that was vehemently against home rule and another that was tacitly trying to support it.

Matters became even worse when violent attacks ensued, which were perpetuated by Irish radicals. One of the most infamous was the Phoenix Park Murders, which occurred in Dublin on May 6th, 1882. Some of the targets in this deadly attack included none other than the newly made chief secretary of Ireland, Lord Frederick Cavendish, and his undersecretary, Thomas Henry Burke.

Having a chief secretary appointed by London was anathema to those who supported home rule. However, for the most part, even the staunchest home rule advocates greeted the news of this atrocity with horror.

Nevertheless, the march toward home rule continued. Even after the death of Parnell in 1891, many of his ideas continued to live on through his supporters. Irish politician John Redmond, in particular, sought to carry forward Parnell's legacy by openly calling for not just home rule but a fully independent Irish republic.

Around this time, another prolific political figure emerged on the Irish landscape: Arthur Griffith. Griffith agreed with many that the Acts of Union passed in 1800 were illegal. Many Irish believed that since no one had consulted the Irish if they wanted to be lumped in with Great Britain that the law should not stand as written.

However, rather than focus his efforts on using parliamentary measures to diminish or even repeal the Acts of Union, Griffith insisted that since the law was illegal and illegitimate, the best thing to do would be to flat-out ignore it. He urged Irish members of Parliament to skip out on British Parliament altogether, instead stating that all Irish elected officials should meet in a local legislative body made up of just Irish representatives. There, they could hash out how to rule Ireland among themselves without any say from England.

Griffith's focus on creating an all Irish legislative body that could shut out the English led to the creation of a political party known as Sinn Fein, which actually translates as "We Ourselves." This party was created in 1905.

The divisive nature of Irish/British relations would continue to simmer until it truly came to a boil when World War One broke out. The extra stress and burden of the First World War truly broke the camel's back as it pertained to the question of home rule for Ireland.

In 1914, Ireland found itself in an interesting position. The world was at war, but the notion of a draft was not popular with the Irish public. Even so, during the course of the conflict, some 200,000 Irish troops would serve in the war, and some 35,000 would be killed. These Irish troops served with distinction during the Gallipoli campaign, which saw British troops stuck in a quagmire in Turkish terrain in the early stages of the war.

Back in Ireland, a vociferous call for home rule had once again ensued. Legislation to allow some semblance of home rule to take shape was established on September 18th, 1914, but it was decided that any further enactment of it would be put off until the war had concluded.

However, that was not enough for many Irish activists. In the middle of the war, on April 24th, 1916 (Easter Monday), a group of radicals seized government facilities in Dublin and called for Irish independence. This uprising of Irish nationalists would go down in history as the Easter Rising.

England responded by declaring martial law the day after the uprising began. Over the next few days, tens of thousands of British troops swarmed in and sought to destabilize a growing—and considering the state of wartime Britain—very much unwanted crisis. A state of war between England and Ireland existed. British troops set up artillery and pounded the locations where the Irish rebels were holed up. The rebels ended up surrendering on April 29th, having to deal with a large number of casualties. After some six days, the crisis was over, with hundreds dead, thousands wounded, and most of Dublin destroyed.

It is surprising how little this footnote of World War One is mentioned, but Britain essentially had to fight a brief war in its own backyard while their troops were embroiled in the trenches. It certainly was not a good feeling for anyone involved. Matters would become even worse when the victorious English decided it would be a good idea to execute many of the prisoners.

Despite the trouble caused by the Irish militants, this incident created a lot of sympathy for the Irish plight. An Irish member of Parliament named John Dillon gave a famous speech on May 11th condemning the action. Dillon stated, "It is not murderers who are being executed; it is insurgents who have fought a clean fight, however misguided, and it would be a damned good thing for you if your soldiers were able to put up as good a fight as did these men in Dublin."[10]

The immediate aftermath of the debacle also managed to shine more light on the Irish organization called Sinn Fein. Although a fringe group, Sinn Fein gained attention for supporting the Easter Rising. After the uprising, almost all of the radicals—whether it was true or not—were

---

[10] Gibney, John. *A Short History of Ireland: 1500-2000*. 2017.

lumped into the Sinn Fein category. Interestingly enough, Arthur Griffith, the founder of the Sinn Fein Party, would be arrested in the immediate aftermath of the Easter Rising, even though there was nothing (besides perhaps his political rhetoric) directly connecting him to the insurrection.

Further developments in 1918 would lead to even more drama. After German troops on the Western Front threatened Allied progress, the British began to institute a draft in Ireland for the first time.

It seemed that the Irish were fine with sending troops in droves when it was on a voluntary basis, but they openly balked at serving in the war when it was deemed to be some sort of fulfillment of a required duty to the United Kingdom.

The Irish, who were still feeling just about as disenfranchised as ever despite any legislative progress that had supposedly been made, could not countenance that they were being forced to fight for a country that they themselves did not feel they were a part of. Many of the more frustrated Irish began to look toward Sinn Fein in earnest. The Irish Volunteers also began to throw their weight behind Sinn Fein, and soon they would come to form what would be dubbed the Irish Republican Army or IRA for short.

The IRA would take on terrorist characteristics. In 1919, a couple of British officials were killed by two radicals named Dan Breen and Sean Treacy, who claimed to be operating under the agency of the Irish Republican Army. By the following year, the IRA and Sinn Fein had become increasingly active.

Rising to lead the movement was an American born, Irish ideologue descended from a Spanish father and an Irish mother. His name was Eamon de Valera.

De Valera was incredibly active during the unrest of 1916. By 1917, he was a leading figure in Sinn Fein, becoming the president. Sinn Fein was positioning itself as a champion for the cause of independence during the postwar era. And sure enough, in the general election of December 1918, Sinn Fein managed to win seventy-three seats in the British Parliament, which was a great achievement for any political party, especially one with as much at stake as Sinn Fein. However, there was much talk of electoral cheating at the time, and even Sinn Fein supporters openly admitted to malfeasance at the ballot box. As it pertains to potential fraud in the 1918 election, writer and historian Peter

Neville spoke of the phenomenon of "impersonation."

According to Neville, it was common for Irish political activists to study the electoral register in advance in order to find names of people who had passed away but were still on the voting rolls. People often laugh whenever accusations are floated that the dead may have voted in an election, but according to Peter Neville, this happened in Ireland's 1918 election.

Neville claims that political hacks took down the names of dead people still on the voting rolls and then sent out agents to "impersonate" them. These agents would then vote on behalf of the dead. As Neville put it, "Sinn Feiners were very good at this, and some claimed to have done it six times in 1918. There were even stories about people doing it twenty times!"[11]

These newly elected members ultimately refused to take their seats in Westminster and instead formed a parliament of their own in Dublin. These newly elected representatives would first convene on January 21st, 1919. On that same day, they declared Irish independence.

Like it or not, Sinn Fein had become a bulwark of opposition against those who did not wish to cut Ireland loose. By 1920, Sinn Fein was in control of the Irish government, controlling most of the local apparatus. Despite claims of election fraud, Sinn Fein seemed to have been supported by most of the Irish people.

The British authorities tried to strike back by unleashing a torrent of what has been described as draconian legislation. This included the formation of a paramilitary unit called the Black and Tans, whose members wore a hodgepodge of police and military ("black and tan") gear. These troops roamed the streets attempting to enforce the state of martial law that much of Ireland had been placed under. As one can imagine, having an occupying force on Irish soil did nothing to make the Irish think any fonder of the British Crown.

On the contrary, the Black and Tans bullied and attacked Irish civilians for something as small as violating curfew. Homes and businesses were burned, and people were killed or injured. Sinn Fein continued to stoke the outrage from the seats of their shadow parliament assembly, which convened in violation of British law.

---

[11] Neville, Peter. *A Traveller's History of Ireland.* 1992.

It should not be too surprising to hear that Sinn Fein would attempt to create its own legislative body with the Irish as representatives since Sinn Fein means "We Ourselves." Proponents of Sinn Fein furthermore viewed the British takeover during the Acts of Union as illegal. Therefore, British authority in Ireland was not legitimate. As much as the British cried foul, Sinn Fein insisted that it was the British who were violating the rights of the Irish.

In many ways, the British troops sent to Ireland were fighting a losing battle from the very beginning. First and foremost, the British troops were viewed as an occupying force, and the Irish rebels were viewed as freedom fighters. The British soldiers were in hostile territory, being thwarted at every step, while their antagonists were on friendly home terrain in which they could easily disperse, hide, and gain support before coordinating their next strike.

Many often cite America's war in Vietnam as an unpopular one, in which the Americans fought not only an official army but also the sentiment of the Vietnamese people who wished to drive them out. But this is only half-true. Yes, some Vietnamese villagers sided with the communists, but not all of them. US troops still had most of South Vietnam ostensibly on their side as they fought the communist forces of North Vietnam. However, the British in Ireland, besides a smattering of Protestants around Dublin, were largely outnumbered and surrounded by Irish Catholics who were hostile to their presence in the region.

Making matters worse was the fact that the British occupying forces came to regard the average citizen as "the enemy." Neither the British troops, whose job it was to patrol Irish streets, nor Irish citizens felt safe. Irish families lived in fear of that "midnight knock" on their door by British soldiers searching for weapons or IRA operatives.

The attempt of the Irish to shake loose of Britain's increasingly harsh grip would be fought until 1921. At the end of this war, the Ango-Irish Treaty (not to be confused with another later treaty of the same name) was put forth. This treaty sought to establish Ireland as a free state and a dominion inside what was known as the British Commonwealth.

The Irish Free State came into effect on December 6th, 1921. The state that came into being was not a republic but a constitutional monarchy with elected representatives in the British Parliament. With this dominion status, the Irish Free State had general independence in governing its own affairs, but the British monarchy remained the ultimate executive authority.

This meant Ireland would be very similar to Canada, which was another British dominion that had gradually worked its way toward independence. However, the Irish were not content. Soon after the treaty for a free state went into effect, two factions of the Irish began fighting each other over their interpretations of what independence really meant.

The Irish Civil War started in Dublin, and it was fought between those who supported the treaty and the anti-treaty IRA. This war would be waged during 1922 and 1923.

The first phase had the anti-Treatyites (the IRA), who were led by Rory O'Connor, take control of the Four Courts. The building was then besieged by the Free Staters led by Michael Collins. Collins's group waylaid the anti-Treatyites with heavy artillery, pushing them out.

There were more anti-Treatyite forces in Cork, but the Free Staters successfully sent forces by sea to confront them. The Free Staters would triumph but at the cost of many lives, including the life of thirty-two-year-old Michael Collins. Collins was gunned down by a group of disgruntled anti-Treatyites in August 1922.

The Irish Civil War fizzled out in early 1923, and the Free Staters were seen as the victors. With de Valera at its head, the Free State of Ireland had been created.

There was a very big catch in all of this because not all of Ireland was given this free-state status. The northeastern corner of the island, which had been the most thoroughly subjected to plantations and all of the other efforts of Anglicization and Protestant proselytizing, would remain linked to the rest of the United Kingdom. The Protestant majority of Northern Ireland wished this to be the case, though.

In 1973, a referendum was held to see whether the majority of people approved leaving the United Kingdom and joining the Republic of Ireland. The vote was boycotted by nationalists, which led to Northern Ireland staying in the United Kingdom.

Map of Ireland today.
https://commons.wikimedia.org/wiki/File:Ei-map.svg

Northern Ireland would remain a lasting sore spot and point of contention for everyone involved. The continued perceived disenfranchisement of Catholics by the Protestants would only make their disapproval more glaring.

It had been a long, hard fight for freedom, but little did anyone know the troubles that awaited the Irish in the years ahead.

# Chapter 8: The Troubles: A Turbulent Relationship

*"They won't break me because the desire for freedom, and the freedom of the Irish people, is in my heart. The day will dawn when all the people of Ireland will have the desire for freedom to show. It is then that we will see the rising of the moon."*

*-Bobby Sands*

There is a tendency in histories about Ireland to move straight from independence and the end of the Irish Civil War in 1923 to the time of the "Troubles," which began in the 1960s. Although these are two high-water marks in Irish history, there is obviously much that went on between those two historical markers. So, having said that, it would do us some good to go over them briefly.

Immediately after Irish independence was achieved, the most important thing for the Irish was to make sure they were able to maintain a solid economic footing. This would become quite difficult after the stock market crash of 1929. Although this event began in the United States, the crash would send shockwaves all over the world.

The Great Depression, as it would be called, would sink its teeth deep into Ireland by the 1930s, but it would be Northern Ireland that faced the full brunt of this economic devastation. Not since the days of the potato famine were times that tough. And since England had been thoroughly lambasted for supposedly not stewarding the Irish through such calamities before, it became doubly important for homegrown Irish administrators to find successful ways to weather their nation through the storm.

One of the biggest hurdles was simply finding jobs for everyone. By the 1930s, six counties of Ireland were being greatly impacted by unemployment, which was around 25 percent.

One may think that such suffering could bring unity to Ireland through the shared experience of universal hardship. However, as it pertained to Irish Catholics and Irish Protestants, this was not the case. Although the people in Ireland were glad to be free and independent, most still carried some form of an ancestral grudge against "the other."

This could be seen in the 1930s when a disturbance was created by an Irish Catholic gardener who worked at the Parliament compound at Stormont and was fired simply because of his own background. The man was a good worker and a veteran of World War One. He had served with distinction. But for those who despised his faith and saw everything through a jaded sectarian lens, such things did not seem to matter.

In the midst of this increasingly volatile situation, the Free State of Ireland forged a new constitution in 1937, which transformed it into the Republic of Ireland. The constitution reaffirmed some basic aspirations of Irish patriots, such as making the Irish tongue the official language of Ireland. Such things were fairly predictable developments.

Less predictable was the fact that this constitution achieved some rather interesting feats of political sleight of hand. For one thing, it actually staked a claim for Ireland controlling all thirty-two counties while admitting the reality that its jurisdiction is only over twenty-six counties. Even so, the wording of the constitution purposefully left the door open for possible future repatriation. This, of course, did not sit well with the Unionists in Northern Ireland.

It was the start of a very turbulent relationship, for lack of better words. In the backdrop of all of this uncertainty, the Second World War erupted. In many ways, the British, in general, and the Irish, in particular, were still getting over the First World War.

In 1939, shortly after Germany's invasion of Poland and the start of the conflict, most Irish had to decide where they stood in the conflagration. They most certainly were not going to take the side of the Germans, but they did not want to be dragged into the conflict by the British either. To most Irish, a stance of neutrality seemed to be the only viable option available.

President de Valera denounced Germany's aggression but also made it clear that Ireland would remain neutral during the conflict. This was not altogether pleasing for Britain, but it was something the British were willing to—at least grudgingly—accept for the time being.

However, being neutral created its own set of problems. If aircraft, for example, were shot down or landed in Ireland, what were the Irish to do? The question of what to do with prisoners of war showed who Ireland was truly aligned with. If any Germans crash-landed in Ireland, they were interned, while Allied service members who landed were quietly transported to England.

Northern Ireland, however, was another matter entirely. Since Northern Ireland was part of the United Kingdom, it was an active participant in the war. Northern Ireland ended up being a staging ground for arriving American troops. A large number of US troops were stationed there during the war.

Interestingly, Northern Ireland made the most progress from an economic standpoint after the war. From 1945 to 1968, Northern Ireland made vast improvements in monetizing assets from agriculture and livestock. Northern Ireland went through a veritable export boom, in which livestock and other agricultural products were shipped to the rest of Great Britain.

Even so, unemployment was still a fairly heavy burden to bear, and it was the Irish Catholics who bore the brunt of it. Historians believe many of these issues were not done intentionally, but the downtrodden of Northern Ireland saw things differently. These hardships were often viewed as being part of a concerted larger plot to actively oppress Irish Catholics.

In this tense backdrop of suspicion, decisions that might have seemed rather innocuous at first glance, such as placing a new university in the Protestant town of Coleraine rather than Catholic Londonderry (or Derry), took on a whole new meaning. In light of these growing misgivings, support for the IRA in Northern Ireland began to pick up speed.

As hostilities began to boil over, Northern Ireland, in particular, began to enter a period widely known as the Troubles. This turbulent period, which spanned from the 1960s to the 1990s, would see instability, strife, turmoil, and bloodshed as the Irish in Northern Ireland struggled to find their footing and their identity.

Contrary to popular opinion, not all of the Irish in the north who were seeking change wanted to make progress through bloodshed or the use of force. In the 1960s, there was a growing nonviolent civil rights movement in Northern Ireland. This organization was known as the Northern Ireland Civil Rights Association (NICRA), and much of the rhetoric and strategies of this movement were patterned off of the American civil rights movement.

The group was founded in February 1967. There were many parallels between the NICRA and America's civil rights movement, but one of the most disturbing was how both groups were often met with violent police action.

On October 5th, 1968, for example, several marchers were stopped as they tried to pass through Londonderry (also known as Derry). These peaceful demonstrators were smashed into by the Royal Ulster Constabulary (RUC). The RUC was the designated police force of Northern Ireland, which was almost entirely Protestant in its makeup.

At this point in time, there were many Catholics in Northern Ireland who believed that the only solution was to separate from the United Kingdom outright. The largely Protestant majority who disagreed wanted to stay and were known as "Unionists."

This contentious situation came to a head in the summer of 1969. That August, the Unionists launched a series of vicious assaults on Catholic neighborhoods in Belfast and Londonderry. The situation seemed dire, and all eyes were on the leadership (or lack thereof) of the Unionists of Northern Ireland, led by North Ireland's prime minister, James Chichester-Clark.

When local governance did not seem to be up to the challenge of keeping the peace, British troops began to show up in force. It was not long before the heavy-handed tactics of the British army inflamed sentiments in Northern Ireland.

First, a harsh curfew was put in place in July 1970. This was not popular with anyone, and the harsh manner in which it was enforced was only bound to cause trouble. Something even worse happened the following summer, in August of 1971. Irish Catholic neighborhoods were targeted for internment. Much of Northern Ireland exploded in violent riots. During a particularly bad spate of rioting, twenty-two people died, and countless others were forced out of their neighborhoods due to the wanton destruction that had ensued.

It was around this point that the IRA (Irish Republican Army) is said to have been revitalized. The IRA was increasingly seen by many Irish Catholics as not a radical group but the actual guardians and protectors of the Irish Catholic way of life. Essentially, the only thing standing between the Irish Catholics and certain destruction at the hands of the Unionists and the British army was the IRA.

The IRA had two ideological wings, one that leaned left and one that leaned right. These two wings first crystallized on January 11th, 1970, during a Dublin meeting of IRA representatives when the Official IRA decided to continue the struggle through political means. The more radical right-wing group known as the Provisional IRA splintered off and set itself on a much more militant and confrontational path.

This group called themselves "Provisional" in reference to the Provisional Government of Dublin, which had gone into effect in 1916. The Provisionals (often referred to in slang as "Provos") accused the Official IRA of being leftist and even Marxist in character. But most importantly, the Provos disagreed with the Official IRA's nonviolent stance.

The Provisional IRA believed they were well past the time for talk and deliberation and that force was indeed necessary. This confrontational approach was on full display in the spring of 1970. In remembrance of the Easter Rising that had occurred several decades prior, violent demonstrations were held by the Provisional IRA.

The use of heavy-handed tactics by the British during the unrest of 1971, most especially the internment of Irish Catholics, played into the hands of IRA belligerents of all stripes. The British had provided Irish Catholics all the reason in the world to look up to the Provisional IRA for support. The Provisional IRA (sometimes referred to as Provos) declared that the only solution to the problems facing Northern Ireland was to sever ties with the United Kingdom.

The Unionist Protestants of Northern Ireland, of course, did not agree, so the dilemma continued. This dilemma reared its ugly head in a terrible way in 1972 when a group of British paratroops massacred a group of thirteen Irish Catholic civil rights advocates in Londonderry. This incident, known as Bloody Sunday, would firmly put the Irish Catholics on the side of the IRA.

The Official IRA would soon take action as well, with several coordinated attacks being launched on British targets. It would later be learned that the IRA entered into a bargain with none other than Libyan dictator Muammar Gaddafi in 1972. Gaddafi, who at one time aided a multitude of militants all over the globe, decided it was in his interest to aid the IRA to provoke the British.

By now, the Troubles were in full swing. Right on the heels of the events of Bloody Sunday, the parliamentary doors of Northern Ireland were closed. In its place, a new agreement was hashed out that would have both Protestant and Catholic representatives engage in a power-sharing arrangement in the form of a consensus government. However, this arrangement strongly favored the Protestants in Dublin and was soon denounced by Irish Catholics.

Ultimately, the Official IRA managed to come to terms, and a ceasefire was eventually arranged in 1972. The Provisional IRA would keep on fighting.

The Provisional IRA revved up its attacks and soon would even reach into England. In 1974, IRA militants targeted and attacked Birmingham. These actions had some calling British Birmingham "British Bombingham."

Ireland was going through a terrible inflation crisis during part of this period. Much of this was kicked off by the oil embargo of 1973, which led to inflated oil prices in much of the world. As is so often the case, when the price of oil and gas went up, so did the price of food, which had to be transported by trucks that were suffering at the pump over the inflated gas prices.

There was a decisive uptick in violence during this time. Between 1973 and 1976, random people were killed, and buildings were demolished in terrorist attacks. A series of bombings reached all the way into England itself, gaining much attention in 1973. Furthermore, it is said that over two hundred people were killed on average each year thereafter, with the most being killed in 1976. In 1976, a whopping 297 were killed as a result of the political upheaval in Northern Ireland.

That fateful year of 1976 saw the IRA massacre ten random Protestants in revenge for six Irish Catholics who had been previously killed. This bloody incident, known as the Kingsmill massacre, was soon followed by an event that managed to get even more attention. A UK ambassador, along with a fellow civil servant, were blown up after crossing a landmine in Dublin.

However, the most damning incident happened in August of that year when a supposed IRA Provo militant was shot by British troops during a high-speed chase. The militant ended up crashing his stolen vehicle and killing a few kids in Belfast. This sad incident led Mairead Corrigan, the aunt of one of the kids who were killed, to team up with fellow activist Betty Williams to lead a massive peace demonstration. They demanded all sides put a stop to the violence.

The most important political gesture during this period was the end of the highly controversial practice of internment. However, the end of internment also brought about the end of the United Kingdom viewing those who remained in custody as political prisoners. Instead, they were viewed as just regular run-of-the-mill criminals guilty of crimes against the state. This move was highly criticized by IRA supporters since it meant they would lose many rights and distinctions they had previously held under the designation of political prisoners.

This led to vehement protests by Irish prisoners being held in UK custody throughout the rest of the 1970s and into the early 1980s. The protests began in a rather simple but straightforward manner. The prisoners initially refused to wear the clothes given to them that signaled they were normal prisoners. Instead, these prisoners of war wrapped blankets around themselves while shrugging off any official prison uniforms they were given.

When this failed to get the desired results, they increased their pressure campaign by refusing to get out of their cells. They would not even leave to use the bathroom. Feces and urine soon covered their living space. This rather nasty episode became known as the "dirty protest." This form of protest did get attention, but it did not get the desired result of having the prisoners recognized as political detainees.

By 1980, the prisoners had changed tactics and had decided to embark upon a general hunger strike instead. The group was quite serious about it and refused to give up until their demands were met.

One young man who was part of the hunger strike proved just how serious he was when he literally starved himself to death. That young man was named Bobby Sands, and he would go down as a martyr for the cause of the IRA.

Making matters more interesting, right before Bobby Sands perished, he was actually elected as a member of Parliament. This meant that

British Prime Minister Margaret Thatcher had basically refused to give any ground whatsoever to the Irish prisoners, even though one was a member of Parliament.

Thatcher could have cared less if he was a member of Parliament. In her mind, he was a criminal terrorist, and she would not budge one inch to terrorist demands.

In her way of thinking, if Bobby starved, it was his own fault. All he had to do was eat; she was not stopping him from doing so. Even so, many began to view Thatcher as nothing short of a monster for her hardline stance and for not at least attempting to somehow placate the starving twenty-seven-year-old enough to convince him to give up the hunger strike.

The IRA only grew stronger as a result. The propaganda coup brought about by the uncaring prime minister who "let Bobby starve" was great for recruitment.

Sinn Fein once again rose to prominence as well, this time as a well-oiled political machine. The main gears of this machine were IRA stalwarts Gerry Adams, Martin McGuinness, and Danny Morrison. The mobilization of Sinn Fein proved successful and gained results. This was evident in the election that took place in the fall of 1982, which saw Sinn Fein gaining a full 10 percent of the votes cast. The following year, Gerry Adams secured a seat in Parliament.

But even as some IRA members were seeking results through the ballot box, others were sticking to bullets. In 1979, eighteen British troops were massacred at Warrenpoint. This was followed by the assassination of Louis Mountbatten, 1st Earl of Mountbatten, who was a relative of the British royal family. He was killed while in Ireland during the holidays.

The early 1980s were full of violent acts. In 1984, for example, the IRA bombed a hotel where the Conservatives, including Margaret Thatcher, were meeting. Thatcher just barely managed to escape unscathed.

This stunning incident made it abundantly clear that something had to be done to stop all of this terror and bloodshed. The Anglo-Irish Agreement went into effect on November 15th, 1985, with the official backing of both London and Dublin in an effort to solve the problem of Northern Ireland.

Violence would continue over the next few years. Eleven Protestants were killed during a bloody incident in 1987, and a whopping twenty-seven were murdered in 1993. But even so, efforts were made by both Dublin and London to find a solution. This road map would continue to be followed throughout the 1990s.

The Downing Street Declaration was made in 1993. Overseen by Prime Minister John Major, this declaration stated that the United Kingdom no longer had any real strategic interest in Northern Ireland.

It was further stated that if a majority of those who lived in Northern Ireland voiced an interest in returning to Ireland, the United Kingdom would not stand in their way. This mutual agreement helped lead to an official ceasefire between the Provisional Irish Republican Army and the government of the United Kingdom on August 31$^{st}$, 1994.

Aiding the process was the establishment of the Forum for Peace and Reconciliation, which was put in place by government officials in Dublin in October 1994. This special venue created a platform in which opposing sides could talk and openly air their grievances without any fear of violence or retaliation.

These peaceful overtures would face turbulence in the spring of 1996 when radical factions within the IRA grew impatient with the process. There was also growing fury at the trespasses of an increasingly belligerent Orange Order. As mentioned earlier in this book, the Orange Order is a fraternal Protestant organization.

Irish Protestants were literally on the march in 1996, marching in extravagant parades to show their support for Protestantism and unionism, to the chagrin of local Catholics. When they passed through predominantly Catholic neighborhoods, riots erupted. Local governments felt hamstrung to stop the tumult since the Orangemen (as they were called) insisted that it was their right to march. If the government banned the marches, Irish Protestants would run riot.

In the midst of this tumult and unrest, the IRA decided to strike. On February 9$^{th}$, 1996, these radical militants detonated an explosive device at London's Canary Wharf.

Many had lost faith in Prime Minister Major's efforts by this point, and the following year, 1997, he was voted out in favor of Prime Minister Tony Blair.

Blair seemed determined to patch up the ongoing peace talks. He reached out to his Irish counterpart, Bertie Ahern, and even solicited the aid of United States President Bill Clinton as he attempted to revive the peace talks that had seemingly stalled.

These efforts paid off when another ceasefire was obtained in late 1997, and talks began anew by early 1998. The talks led to the Good Friday Agreement (also known as the Belfast Agreement), which took place on April 10th, 1998. This agreement was hailed by all as the greatest attempt yet to create a lasting peace in Northern Ireland. The agreement called for a devolved assembly in Northern Ireland. This devolved assembly would allow the Unionists and Irish nationalists to have a say in their government in what was viewed as a kind of power-sharing agreement.

The agreement furthermore insisted that violence would be firmly rejected by both sides. The peace agreement was signed on Good Friday, and it seemed as if real progress had been made. However, that did not stop some of the most extreme members of the IRA from conducting one final devastating attack. This occurred in August 1998, just a few months after the agreement had been made, when a car bomb was detonated in the markets of Armagh, resulting in the deaths of twenty-nine people.

The power-sharing portion of the agreement in regard to the devolved assembly was actually revoked in the early 2000s, but it was put back in place in April 2007. Since then, violence in Northern Ireland has fortunately become a much rarer event. The Provisional IRA has ceased functioning as a paramilitary group. So, are the troubles over? We can only hope.

# Chapter 9: The Celtic Tiger: The Economic Boom and Bust

*"What were once only hopes for the future have now come to pass; it is almost exactly 13 years since the overwhelming majority of people in Ireland and Northern Ireland voted in favor of the agreement signed on Good Friday 1998, paving the way for Northern Ireland to become the exciting and inspirational place that it is today."*

*-Queen Elizabeth II*

One of the reasons the peace talks between Ireland and England became more attractive was the fact that there was a sudden uptick in the Irish economy. It was unexpected by most, but by the early 1990s, as moves were being made to start peace talks, the Irish economy had surged with a sudden unexpected boom.

Ireland was even referred to as the "Celtic Tiger" due to its economy's ferocious and unrelenting growth. The term was apparently first used in remarks by industry giant Morgan Stanley. In a 1994 economic report on the region, writer Kevin Gardiner referred to Ireland as a Celtic Tiger in light of its sudden rise. This rise has been compared with the sudden rise of some East Asian states, such as Singapore, Taiwan, and South Korea, all of which were previously referred to as economic "tigers."

This Celtic boom has since been largely attributed to post-Cold War investments by both the United States and the European Union. After the fall of the Soviet Union, the United States seemed poised to be the sole super power on the planet. The United States had the most powerful military and the biggest wallet, and for many, Ireland seemed like prime real estate in which to invest.

The European Union was also quite interested in Ireland since it was a Euro-friendly nation (friendly to both European culture as well as European money) with a ready-made English-speaking workforce that could be tapped for a wide variety of roles. Another incentive for investors was the fact that Ireland boasted a much lower rate for corporate taxes.

For these mega-corporations, Ireland seemed like a great place to buy huge tracts of land and construct factories. Ireland became a manufacturing hub, especially in the emerging tech sector. By 1998, around 40 percent of all of Ireland's exports were involved with computing. Both Dell and Gateway used Ireland as a home base for their operations.

All of these investments in Ireland and its economy led to greatly expanded infrastructure and industry in all sectors. And all of this combined, of course, meant plenty of jobs. Instead of waves of Irish fleeing their home country, expats were now returning. Not only that, people who were not even from Ireland were heading to the island for better opportunities.

Eastern Europeans, especially those from nations that had just joined up or were thinking of joining the European Union, flooded into Ireland. Becoming a desirable destination for one seeking a career was new and uncharted territory for Ireland.

For a while, there was a steady and powerful positive feedback loop in place. Investments allowed for growth in industry, which allowed for jobs, which then gave spending power to the populace, who spent their hard-earned cash at retailers, restaurants, and on real estate. All of this money ultimately circled back to the industries responsible for growth, repeating the cycle all over again.

It sounds all perfectly well and good. So, what happened? Well, since most of the investments in the late 1990s to early 2000s were related to tech industries, Ireland was gravely affected when the dot-com bubble burst.

The bubble was created when the general public became heavily interested in all things tech. Computers were being bought, and the internet was being used by a wide swathe of the public sector for the first time.

The dot-com boom was really no different from many other technology-related booms that have occurred in history. The mass implementation of railroads in the 1840s, for example, had a similar boom, and so did the sudden widespread availability of cars a hundred years later.

Riding these sudden waves of consumer enthusiasm is great while they last, but as it pertains to the dot-com boom, there was a sudden and unexpected slump in the tech industry.

A wide range of theories have been presented as to why this happened, from just general declining interest to companies being way too fearful of the Y2K crisis. Y2K was used to refer to a computer programming shortcut. People feared that the internal clocks in computing systems, which had been originally programmed to run on just two digits to signify the years, would be unable to recognize the year 2000, which, in a two-digit format, would have been reduced to "00."

Whatever the reason, there was a decline in sales, corporations briefly panicked, and the dot-com bubble burst. Thus, investment in Ireland suffered as a result.

Unfortunately for Ireland, the other major moneymaker for the Emerald Isle—tourism—suffered as well after the terrorist attacks on New York City, US, on September 11th, 2001. Because of the attacks, many began to reconsider flying on a plane. The 9/11 attacks saw terrorists slamming commercial planes into New York's World Trade Center, as well as America's military nerve center, the Pentagon. There was a fourth plane, but the hostages on board were able to take it over, crashing the plane into a field in Pennsylvania. No one survived any of the plane crashes. Fear of flying led to a decisive drop in tourism, and Ireland was adversely affected as a result.

Ireland began to somewhat recover by 2003, but there were other problems ahead. Many investors had found that it was much cheaper to take their business to eastern Europe, where the people were not demanding high wages and expensive insurance premiums.

Such decisions would have many corporations pulling stakes out of Ireland and relocating to eastern European countries. Ireland tried to recoup, and some progress was made. Wishful thinkers even began to speak of a potential "Celtic Tiger 2" on the horizon. But then the housing bubble of 2008 burst, and the shockwaves hit Ireland particularly hard.

Ireland had been a big recipient of bank investments into various properties, so once the Irish property bubble burst wide open, Ireland was in dire need of a bailout. A huge amount of GDP (gross domestic product) was used that year to do just that, but the effort led to a terrible recession.

Even so, all of the economic fortunes that Ireland had been subjected to were enough to fundamentally transform key aspects of Ireland and Irish society. The pull toward the European Union, in particular, has had some lasting and perhaps surprising effects. The adoption of the euro as currency has largely been beneficial for Ireland in that it has greatly opened up Irish markets on the world stage.

In order to remain in the European Union, Ireland has to abide by European Union rules, which has led to a transformation of Irish society. Due to European Union, Ireland finally ditched its antiquated practice of having female civil servants dismissed simply because they had gotten married in 1973. This is just one example, but it shows the potential for social change in Ireland due to EU pressure.

Ireland's connections to the Continent allowed the country to quickly become less isolated and much more cosmopolitan in scope. We can only wonder what changes may be in store for Ireland in the very near future.

# Chapter 10: Modern Ireland in the 21st Century

*"On the island of Ireland, the issue of the border is more than just a practical issue. It is about emotion, history and politics."*

*-Penny Mordaunt*

The next phase in Irish economic history was the Celtic recovery, which some have referred to as nothing short of a Celtic phoenix rising from the ashes. The Celtic recovery was kickstarted in 2014 and, over the last several years, has proceeded at a rather steady clip. Ireland's GDP is said to have risen as much as 7 percent by 2015, and favorable trends continued in subsequent years. Ireland continues to boast a low corporate tax rate and a highly educated populace, which are both conducive to the tech industry. This has led to a resurgence of tech firms in the nation, such as Apple, Facebook, and Google. Even so, this rapid boom has made many wonder if Ireland just might again see a bubble bust.

Probably the biggest and most glaring flaw in Ireland's economy is the fact that it relies so much on the investment of multinational companies. Ireland is basically presenting itself as a good place for foreign investments. But what about homegrown industries?

Instead of American-originated Apple, Google, Microsoft. and Facebook, how about an original Irish invention or two? As long as the big multinational companies do well, the investment is there, and Ireland remains in good shape. But should they pull out, the Celtic phoenix will soon burn up into a heap of ash.

We also must not forget the drama of Brexit. Although the United Kingdom (including Northern Ireland) decided to make its exit from the European Union, Ireland itself did not. Even so, special protocols were put in place, the Northern Ireland Protocol to be exact, that would still allow for European Union free movement and for the European Union Customs Union to be in effect to avoid cumbersome and unnecessary problems in the region. However, Northern Ireland remains cut off from the European Union single market.

The major point of contention during this whole ordeal was due to the fact that the United Kingdom and Ireland did not wish to have a hard border. They did not want a hard line between Northern Ireland and the Irish Republic that would be difficult to cross. If one were to look at any situation in the world in which the region of a country has been partitioned, such as East Germany and West Germany, one would realize why such matters are sensitive.

Yes, Northern Ireland is still considered to be United Kingdom territory, and yes, the United Kingdom left the European Union, but the rest of Ireland is still part of the European Union. No one wished to create more problems than there already was by making Northern Ireland a strange non-European Union enclave on the same island as the Republic of Ireland.

There would be no United Kingdom version of the Berlin Wall to separate the borders of Northern Ireland from the rest of Ireland. Instead, borders would be relaxed, and much of the European Union protocols would be recognized in Northern Ireland, even though the nation was technically no longer in the EU.

Many hoped that the continued influence of the European Union and the relaxed borders would ease tensions between Northern Ireland and Ireland. This makes sense since the goal of the EU is to create a system of unified European states. People from the Republic of Ireland, Germany, and France are all part of the European Union. Their vision is of a united Europe in which past petty border distinctions are dissolved, and all are simply Europeans.

Most people in Northern Ireland supported remaining in the European Union. However, this support cut mainly across sectarian lines between Catholics and Protestants. Around 56 percent of people in Northern Ireland wished to remain part of the EU. But of course, even though most in Northern Ireland wished to remain, their voices were drowned out by the larger majority in the United Kingdom, of which Northern Ireland is still a part.

It is quite interesting to contemplate that the relaxing of borders through the European Union led to the Republic of Ireland and Northern Ireland drawing closer together after years of isolation. In the past, most specifically during the time of the Troubles, one had to go through countless military checkpoints just to cross from Northern Ireland to the rest of the island.

The Good Friday Agreement, which brought an end to the violence, began the process of phasing out this previously hard border, a process that was completed in 2005. With both sides now practicing the soft borders prescribed by the EU (even though Northern Ireland is no longer in the EU as of 2024), it is practically just a walk in the park to get to one side or the other. Local Irish and passport-carrying tourists are very thankful for that.

In consideration of all of this, we can only speculate what things may mean in the days ahead. Can the European Union provide a bridge for Northern Ireland to be repatriated back to full Irish control some point before the close of the 21st century?

Interestingly enough, in April 2017, the European Union actually considered this very thing and decreed that if Northern Ireland ever officially unified with the rest of Ireland, it would automatically be considered part of the EU.

Of course, when the 2020 pandemic hit, things changed drastically. Ireland, however, immediately rose to the challenge. Ireland was consistently ranked as one of the top countries as it pertained to how they managed the crisis, especially when it came to getting the public vaccinated.

Ireland was seen as a world leader for how it handled the pandemic while mitigating potential damage to Irish society and the economy. In 2021, Bloomberg.com recognized Ireland as a leading nation for how it handled the storm. The reasoning behind this ranking is said to be due to the fact that Ireland's vaccination rates were among the highest at the time. In other countries, there was a lot of vaccine skepticism and hesitancy, but in Ireland, it seems that most Irish had no qualms about rolling up their sleeves and getting the vaccine.

Ireland might have been a leader during the pandemic, but the country has always been a bit reluctant to lead others on the international stage. For instance, Ireland has tended to remain neutral in military conflicts that have entangled many other nations.

Ireland might have sent volunteers to support the British effort during World War One, but as soon as Ireland became a free state, it made it clear that it desired to remain neutral from that day forward. Ireland was famously neutral during World War Two and has mostly remained so in the major conflicts that have sprung up across the globe.

However, the Russian invasion of Ukraine in the spring of 2022 began to make many in Ireland, as well as those who consider themselves to be Ireland's friends, reconsider. Initially, Ireland stuck to the typical playbook, with Irish Prime Minister Micheal Martin declaring that Ireland fully intended to retain its status as a neutral, non-belligerent nation on February 24th, 2022.

He did allow for a small caveat to this. He insisted that although Ireland would not get involved militarily, it could get involved on a political level. As Prime Minister Micheal Martin put it, "Ireland's official policy is to be militarily non-aligned. We are, however, not politically non-aligned."[12] Still, as of this writing, Ireland has stopped short of offering any kind of direct military aid or assistance.

Ireland has reasons for its neutrality. Ireland is a fairly small country, and its alliances are a bit more complicated than most. Ireland is technically aligned with Britain, but Ireland's relationship with Britain has been a historically difficult one. Thus, there still remains a cautious political (as well as emotional) distance between the two.

During World War Two, the Irish faced invoking the wrath of both the British and the Germans if they were to side too closely with either one. Neutrality was decided to be the most practical policy. Of course, one may argue that neutrality is the easy way out and that there could be a day in which Ireland will have to make a choice.

Some wonder if Ireland is on the verge of making that choice in light of Russia's invasion of Ukraine. In many ways, Ukraine and Ireland are

---

[12] O'Halloran, Marie. "Ireland Is Not Neutral About Ukraine." https://www.irishtimes.com/politics/2022/11/15/ireland-is-not-neutral-about-ukraine-taoiseach-insists-in-renewed-row-over-constitutional-position/.

very similar nations. Ukraine, just like Ireland, has long been bullied by its more powerful neighbor, Russia.

It will be a bit much to go into the whole history of Russian antagonism against Ukraine, but we can at least trace it back to the days of the Russian Empire when wholesale cultural campaigns were forced upon occupied Ukraine. The Russian tsars tried to force Ukrainians to speak Russian and become "Russified." If this sounds an awful lot like Britain's attempt at social engineering in Ireland by installing plantations, you would be right.

The fact that such a small and typically underestimated country like Ireland has gained such worldwide recognition is indeed remarkable. In light of all of these developments in the $21^{st}$ century, one can only speculate what the next few decades may bring. It would be interesting to see a fully unified Ireland by the time the $22^{nd}$ century rolls around. But only time will tell.

# Conclusion: The Resilience and Unity of Ireland

To say that Ireland is a tough and resilient nation is perhaps one of the greatest understatements of all time. The fact that Irish culture, Irish language, Irish music, and other customs remain and are celebrated today is a strong testament to the enduring nature of Irish civilization. If one were to look at the history of how England attempted to insert plantations into Ireland to subsume its character and dramatically change the culture of the region, it is indeed impressive that Ireland has remained a unique civilization outside of England.

Ultimately, the most damage that England did as it pertains to Ireland is in regard to Northern Ireland. A strong divide between Protestants and Irish Catholics was created there. However, these differences have eased with the passage of time. Of course, there are tensions, but the violence over religion is not as prevalent today as it was in the past.

Today, Catholics outnumber Protestants in Northern Ireland. The nation is undergoing a transformation in which the damage of enforced Anglicization is being reversed, and all things Irish are being revitalized. It has been said that the best thing that ever happened to the Republic of Ireland and Northern Ireland was their entry into the European Union, and there are a lot of great arguments that can be made to that point.

The European Union has its critics, of course, but if there was ever any country that benefited the most from the sweeping changes that entry into the EU can provide, it was Ireland, most especially Northern

Ireland.

Suddenly, it seemed as if Northern Ireland was no longer divided from the rest of the island. Without any official unification, it seemed that at least some sense of unity through the EU had been achieved. And the implications are far-reaching. The culture and politics of the two Irelands are starting to blend. By the early 2020s, Sinn Fein had become popular in Northern Ireland. This would have been unthinkable before, yet now, it has become a reality.

Of course, such tidings are not welcome by all. The Unionists are not pleased with Northern Ireland's increasing political ties with the popular political brands of the Republic of Ireland. Some of the more cynical and critical of British politics may even speculate if the British backed out of the European Union and instigated Brexit because Northern Ireland was becoming too close to the Republic of Ireland.

Could it be that the unifying force of the European Union, which managed to unite the entire island of Ireland in ways that were previously deemed impossible, threatened the British worldview that Northern Ireland would always be separate and distinct from the rest of the Emerald Isle? One can only wonder.

To conclude, the resilience of the Irish people is indeed remarkable. Although the Irish have faced countless hardships, one cannot deny their passion and strength.

If you enjoyed this book, a review on Amazon would be greatly appreciated because it would mean a lot to hear from you.

**To leave a review:**
1. Open your camera app.
2. Point your mobile device at the **QR** code.
3. The review page will appear in your web browser.

--------------------------------------------------------------

*Thanks for your support!*

# Here's another book by Enthralling History that you might like

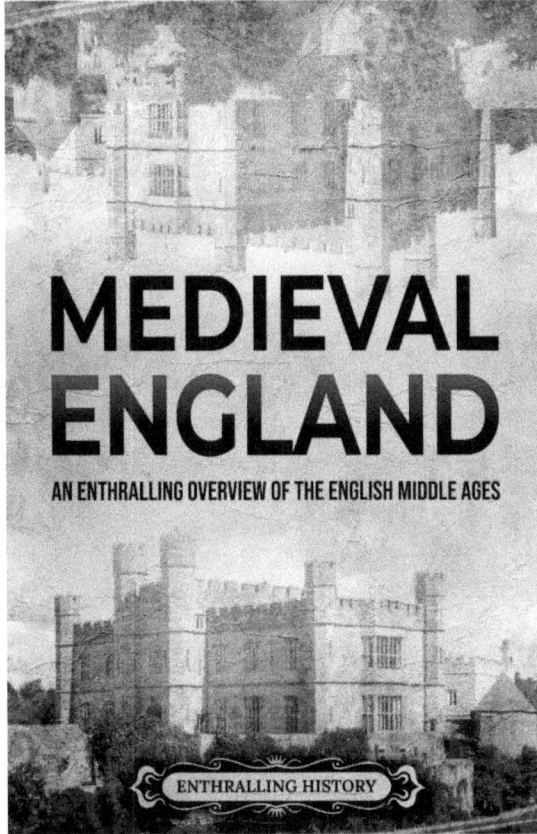

**MEDIEVAL ENGLAND**

AN ENTHRALLING OVERVIEW OF THE ENGLISH MIDDLE AGES

ENTHRALLING HISTORY

# Free limited time bonus

We forget 90% of everything
that we've read in 7 days...

Get the free printable pdf summary of
the book you've read AND much, much
more... shhhh...

Enter Your Most Frequently Used Email to Get Started

**DOWNLOAD FREE PDF
SUMMARY**

© Enthralling History

Stop for a moment. We have a free bonus set up for you. The problem is this: we forget 90% of everything that we read after 7 days. Crazy fact, right? Here's the solution: we've created a printable, 1-page pdf summary for this book that you're reading now. All you have to do to get your free pdf summary is to go to the following website: https://livetolearn.lpages.co/enthrallinghistory/

## Or, Scan the QR code!

Once you do, it will be intuitive. Enjoy, and thank you!

# Appendix A: Further Reading and Reference

Ashley, Mike. *The Giant Book of Myths and Legends.* 1995.

Cronin, Mike. *A History of Ireland.* 2001.

Foster, R. F. *The Oxford Illustrated History of Ireland.* 1989.

Gibney, John. *A Short History of Ireland: 1500-2000.* 2017.

Neville, Peter. *A Traveller's History of Ireland.* 1992.

O'Halloran, Marie. "Ireland Is Not Neutral About Ukraine." https://www.irishtimes.com/politics/2022/11/15/ireland-is-not-neutral-about-ukraine-taoiseach-insists-in-renewed-row-over-constitutional-position/.

Osborne-McKnight, Juilene. *The Story We Carry in Our Bones: Irish History for Americans.* 2015.

State, F. Paul. *A Brief History of Ireland.* 2009.

www.ingramcontent.com/pod-product-compliance
Lightning Source LLC
LaVergne TN
LVHW051754080426
835511LV00018B/3314